GREENING YOUR OFFICE

Strategies That Work

Jill Doucette and Lee Johnson

Self-Counsel Press
(a division of)
International Self-Counsel Press Ltd.
USA   Canada

Self-Counsel Press acknowledges the financial support of the Government of Canada through the Canada Book Fund for our publishing activities.

Printed in Canada.

First edition: 2014

Library and Archives Canada Cataloguing in Publication

Johnson, Lee, 1983- , author
    Greening your office : strategies that work / Lee Johnson and Jill Doucette.

(Self-Counsel green series)
Issued in print and electronic formats.
ISBN 978-1-77040-208-9 (pbk.).—ISBN 978-1-77040-964-4 (epub).—ISBN 978-1-77040-965-1 (kindle)

    1. Business enterprises—Environmental aspects. 2. Business enterprises—Equipment and supplies—Environmental aspects. 3. Office management—Environmental aspects. 4. Social responsibility of business. I. Doucette, Jill, 1986- , author II. Title. III. Series: Self-Counsel green series

HD30.255.J64 2014   658.4'083   C2014-905613-3

Materials provided by Travis Doucette, used with permission.
Materials provided by Vancouver Island Green Business Synergy Sustainability Institute, used with permission.
Materials provided by Monk Office and Debbie Schultz, Executive Assistant to the CEO, used with permission.
Materials provided by Climate Smart, used with permission.
Materials provided by Inn at Laurel Point, used with permission.
Materials provided by Habit Coffee and Shane Devereaux, owner, used with permission.
Materials provided by Level Ground Trading, used with permission.
Materials provided by Metrics Chartered Accountants, used with permission.
Materials provided by Stephen Whipp, Investment Advisor, Stephen Whipp Financial, a Division of Wolverton Securities, used with permission.
Materials provided by Dave Crothall, used with permission.
Matertias provided by Farley Martin Notary Public, used with permission.
Materials provided by Sitka Brand Vision, used with permission.
Materials provided by Oughtred Coffee & Tea and John Oughtred, owner, used with permission.
Materials provided by GeaZone Eco-Courier, used with permission.

Self-Counsel Press
(a division of)
International Self-Counsel Press Ltd.

Bellingham, WA   North Vancouver, BC
USA   Canada

Contents

Notice to Readers

Laws are constantly changing. Every effort is made to keep this publication as current as possible. However, the authors, the publisher, and the vendor of this book make no representations or warranties regarding the outcome or the use to which the information in this book is put and are not assuming any liability for any claims, losses, or damages arising out of the use of this book. The reader should not rely on the authors or the publisher of this book for any professional advice. Please be sure that you have the most recent edition.

Acknowledgments

Thanks to all of the fantastic business owners and managers we have worked with, who have become leaders in business sustainability. Huge thanks to Kayli Anderson, Zack Simon, Chantal Orr, Jessica Iida, Heidi Grantner, Craig Sorochan, Warren Recker, Katherine Murphy, Claire Hume, Linsi Comfort, Joty Dhaliwal, and Lindsay Doucette. Without your contributions and hard work, this book would not have been possible. Thanks also to Travis Doucette for many of the graphic illustrations.

Thanks to Kirk LaPointe and the Self-Counsel Press team for the opportunity; and to Eileen Velthuis, Tanya Lee Howe, and Dr. Tricia Lee for your extraordinary editing skills.

1
Why Go Green at the Office?

More than 7 billion people exist on this planet. Innovations in technology, energy production, medicine, and education have taken us to great heights, but our demand for resources has severe consequences. Since the industrial revolution, we have seen millions of hectares of forest converted to crops, ocean acidification due to global warming, and the permanent loss of many species including birds, frogs, and dolphins. Without a doubt, we are in need of change towards a more sustainable future for all generations.

Major environmental issues we face today can be tackled in the way we live, play, and work. The planet needs leaders. Your office is a great place to make changes and start leading.

1. *What Is a Green Office?*

A green office is one that seeks to limit the amount of environmental resources that are used to conduct business. In the process of reducing its environmental impact, a business can reduce costs, increase staff morale, and enhance brand image. No matter what your organization, business, or group is, there are many easy and affordable ways your office can go green.

The office has become a common work environment. We are all familiar with its basic composition: computers, lighting, paper, printers, desks, and coffee (lots and lots of coffee). Think of the vast amount of offices in the world, or even your city. If every office printed less, reduced energy use, and bought fair-trade coffee, the global impact would be massive!

Moving towards a green office starts with perspective. Looking at your office from a triple-bottom-line framework of People, Planet, and Profit can help you discover opportunities to make positive changes that benefit your business, the community, and the environment. This framework will be discussed in detail in Chapter 2.

Often the most effective way to kick off the green initiative is by designating a green champion within your office to facilitate the process and find solutions that are the best fit for your workplace and budget. You can then create a set of common goals for going green in your office. Goal setting can come in many forms, from general office staff who want to see the office's operational practices change to the management level which may be a part of a larger initiative. Improving your office's environmental performance can help your organization become an environmental leader.

There is no cookie-cutter solution for creating a green office, but there is a general approach that we offer, which has worked for offices with 5 employees and offices with 300 employees. The approach developed by Synergy Enterprises includes four phases of greening a business: Assess, Engage, Implement, and Market. We will explain the details of these phases in Chapter 5.

This book will provide you with a simple and straightforward guide for greening your office, interlaced with real case studies and examples from other offices. You will find that there is a great business case for greening your office and many simple actions that can lead to big impacts.

2. Why Should Your Office Go Green?

Leading businesses and organizations are pursuing green office efforts because it can help them identify cost savings, build employee morale, and help them reduce their environmental footprint (a measure of the environmental impact that a defined organization has based on the natural resources that it uses and the amount of harmful gases that they produce as a result of its operations). Over the past ten years business practices have shifted focus by balancing social, economic, and environmental performance while maintaining and often improving the businesses' bottom line. Not all efforts in going green will result in an immediate cash payback; however, some efforts will help you reduce the amount of goods that you consume (e.g., products, energy, and water) which will reduce your operating costs and, if marketed correctly, can help raise consumer awareness about the actions your office is taking.

When we consider the amount of energy, water, paper, stationery, and other products that an office can consume as well as the impact of creating, transporting, using, and disposing of these goods, it is easy to see that offices play a major role in reducing the impact on the environment. Reducing the amount of waste that your office generates need not be consuming or difficult. Often all it takes is an education program that seeks to change office behaviors. These programs should be made fun, inclusive, and involve some friendly competition to keep things interesting. Offices can also help reduce their environmental impact by selecting office equipment and products that have improved performance (more on this in Chapter 8).

3. What Are the Benefits?

The main reason to go green in your office is to help improve the state of the environment. Whether your motivation comes as a result of a local initiative or global incident, we hope this book will inspire you with a set of quick and easy solutions and some ways to tackle the bigger issues that you may be facing in your organization's quest to save the planet!

There are many positive spin-offs that can follow a green initiative, which includes improving your bottom line and your brand image as well as giving back to your community. While we will go into more detail in Chapter 4, here is a quick overview of benefits in the following sections.

3.1 Saving money

In many ways, going green is about gaining efficiencies and using resources wisely. Even the smallest behavior change in the office, such as turning off lights and computers, can reduce your annual energy costs. Video conferencing is an easy way to save time, money, and the environment because globally air travel is the largest source of greenhouse gas (GHG) emissions for office-based businesses (Source: Climate Smart, "Offices and Carbon Emissions:

A Climate Smart Industry Brief"). You can also save money with green office products that are durable, refillable, and repairable.

Many businesses are already taking advantage of cost savings such as these. For your endeavor to go green and be sustainable, it is key to find opportunities to reduce costs. Some businesses calculate these savings and create a green fund to pay for future green initiatives that may come at a premium, or have a slow return on investment.

3.2 Improving your brand image

Businesses that want to make meaningful connections with their clients and consumers are looking for ways to go green and improve their public image. A growing base of consumers resonate with businesses that are conscious of their environmental footprint. Having your organizational values align with those of your clients and consumers will help build your brand and increase your marketing reach. Strong environmental values have also been found to attract skilled employees and improve their commitment to being a part of your workplace.

3.3 Giving back to your community

Going green in the office can help support local nonprofits and organizations that are working on environmental conservation and social well-being. Whether you want to give directly to an environmental organization or support a local event, you will help build awareness about these groups while supporting and connecting to their causes. Community events and organizations not only have a direct impact in your community but they can also be very effective in generating positive news articles and stories with which your business will be associated.

2
People, Planet, Profit: Balancing the Triple-Bottom-Line

In the conventional capitalism model, businesses care about the environment and society only to the degree in which they may impact profits. Today, a great awareness of the interconnected global marketplace, finite natural resources, and the role businesses can play in making positive change in our world has given rise to new business models. A triple-bottom-line approach to business not only considers profit, but society and the natural environment as well. This approach seeks to account for all of the impacts that result from your office, beyond (but inclusive of) maximizing profits. This places equal weight on environmental and social impacts, which can be built into your decision making and accounting.

It may seem difficult to balance all of these additional considerations and still be profitable but in many cases working to balance People, Profit, and the Planet can simplify your decision making by providing a guideline for operations, purchasing, hiring, and other changes within your business.

To keep accountable to the triple-bottom-line, you will need to determine your key performance indicators for the three categories in said triple-bottom-line: People, Planet, and Profit. Likely, you already have this sorted for the Profit category: gross revenue, gross profit, net profit, and year-end balance — these are all key performance indicators in the profit category. For the People and Planet categories, you will need to choose which indicators will work best for your company. Use and track these metrics in your year-end accounting, as you would track your profits and retained earnings. We recommend starting with a few simple measures and adding more over time to get a complete picture of your triple-bottom-line. Deciding to incorporate environmental and social metrics and putting them on the same pedestal as profits is a critical step towards shifting from a profit-driven business to one that is responsible for your a triple-bottom-line.

Once you have determined your triple-bottom-line metrics, your office can create a baseline from which to benchmark future performance. With a solid baseline, you will be able to better understand the impact of the changes made in your office. A baseline will include measures on how your operations impact water and air quality, the amount of energy consumed, the products you purchase, and the waste that is generated over time. Creating a baseline may seem daunting at first but it is instrumental in determining the results of your hard work, and there are simple ways to do it. First, let's look at the different metrics that are possible for People, Planet, and Profit.

1. People

When considering how your operations affect people in your community or workplace there are many high-level measures that are used in governments to understand the overall health of the social system within which your organization is located. Although many of these variables and measures are found at the national, state or provincial, and regional levels it is helpful to know these for your region. Some examples of the high-level indicators of social well-being for the society surrounding your business include:

- Participation in social activities.
- Charitable donations.

- Volunteering.
- Unemployment rate.
- Education.
- Median household income.
- Life expectancy.
- Average commute time.

This is by no means a complete list but it should give you a better sense of how social well-being in your community can be measured. How does this relate to your office? An office can help facilitate social well-being amongst its staff and customers in a variety of ways. One example is by encouraging your staff to volunteer a certain amount of time annually. Maybe you want to hold a day of litter pick-up on your local waterway, or spend time volunteering in your local soup kitchen. Regardless of which activity you pick, you can help incentivize volunteering by providing staff with the opportunity to do so on staff time, or by making it simple for them to get involved by organizing a team event.

Another example is supporting staff education and training which can have a positive impact on the employability of your staff in the future, median household income, and much more. It is also well acknowledged that workplaces that are committed to balancing their triple-bottom-line improve staff morale, productivity, and engagement. Some simplified measures of social performance in your office may be the following:

- Annual volunteer hours.
- Corporate charity cash donations.
- In-kind or pro bono services and/or products.
- Professional development and/or education hours.
- Internal promotions.
- Nonprofit memberships or partnerships.
- Average employee wages.
- Survey results of employee satisfaction and teamwork.

Decide which measures are appropriate for your company and make a plan to assess your office's performance on an annual basis, as you would assess your year-end or tax payments.

2. Planet

There is an abundance of measures that can help you better understand the amount of natural resources that your organization uses in its operations. A typical office requires transportation to work and meetings, electronics, a space that is heated and cooled, plumbing as well as paper, stationery, and other office products.

Your organization can start small or in targeted areas to take action. For example, your business could aim to increase water conservation by 50 percent and focus on reducing water used in toilets, kitchen and bathroom sinks, dishwashers, and outdoor watering. Here are some examples of a green office's key environmental performance indicators:

- Energy consumption.
- Water consumption.
- Fuel use for business travel.
- Paper purchased.
- Total garbage, recyclables, and composted waste.
- Percentage of ENERGY STAR®-rated electronics and appliances.
- Percentage of green-certified office products.

Thinking "bigger picture," you may want to calculate your carbon footprint to measure the greenhouse-gas emissions that enter the atmosphere as a result of your office's operations. These will likely include carbon, methane, and nitrogen oxides. The most common air pollutant that is responsible for climate change comes from human emissions of carbon dioxide. Carbon dioxide is generated from most forms of electricity generation and the combustion of fossil fuels. There are even carbon dioxide emissions embedded in the products you purchase as the manufacturing process consumes electricity and the transportation of these goods to your office. You can read more about calculating your carbon footprint in Chapter 9.

3. Profit

One of our goals is to dispel the myth that a green office will cost more to operate. In fact, the opposite is possible. Your business can considerably reduce costs by going green. Businesses we have worked with have reduce expenses up to 20 percent by reducing energy, moving to digital record keeping, and reducing waste. The cost of fuel and electricity is not going to go down in the foreseeable future and as such, the changes you make now can result in even greater savings in the future.

Regardless of where you want to start your efforts, it is important to complete a scan of your existing operations to identify the inefficiencies that may exist. This will also help you find those that require simple solutions that can be implemented immediately. Let's say that your office has ten staff members and you spend $10,000 annually on print paper. You may see this expense as a necessary cost of doing business. However, if you are trying to reduce your environmental impact, you will want to look at using less paper and sourcing paper with recycled content. You may decide to make two changes:

1. Start purchasing 30 percent post-consumer recycled paper, which costs 20 percent more per ream. (You will now pay $12,000 annually for the same amount of paper.)

2. You are going to require all printers default to double-sided. (This will reduce the amount of paper you need to use by a third, or $3,300.) The change to 30 percent post-consumer recycled paper can be paid for by the savings from making the print settings default to double-sided, and still save the office $1,300 annually.

Early adopters of green practices will enjoy the added benefit of changing their operations in advance of any existing environmental legislation which may also put them at a competitive advantage.

If you continually make smart financial decisions on your road to becoming a green company, your office will have the resources to maintain and grow your green program.

There is much to consider when beginning to integrate a triple-bottom-line, and this book will help you understand practical ways to move your business down this path. Next, let's look at some of the barriers you may encounter as your office goes green and discuss strategies to overcome them.

3
Common Barriers to a Green Office

In North America, the majority of businesses are small, owner-operated companies. They manage cash flow, customers, staff, janitors, advertising, sales systems, negotiations, leases, inventory, payroll — the list is seemingly endless. Of all the reasons we have heard from business owners about why they haven't gone green, the main one is that it is something else to worry about. "I would love to, but I have an ever perpetuating to-do list of important items," said Joan, a busy office manager of a financial firm. Nearby, in a local law office, a partner told me, "I don't know who would take this on, no one has the time."

In a constant state of competing priorities, it can be hard to think about going green. Our goal is to assure you that going green is a worthwhile endeavor. Both the law and financial firms mentioned have since taken action and reaped both financial and environmental benefits. Healthier employees, a stronger brand, cost savings, and the comfort and pride that your company is making the right choices for the planet — these are all great reasons to tackle going green. There are four major barriers that businesses face in the process: Time, Authority, Cash, and Knowledge (TACK). See Figure 1 and consider how these barriers may impact your business.

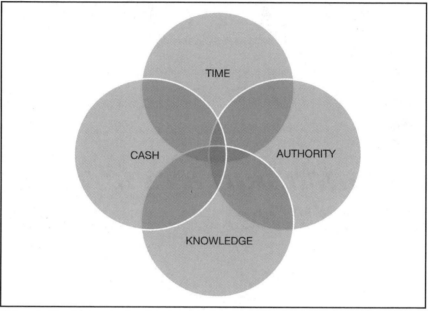

Figure 1: The four major barriers to greening your business.

1. Barrier 1: Time

Time is money, so we need to make sure that the time we spend going green is efficient and impactful.

With a little structure, you can have an effective green program in your office that doesn't take a lot of time to manage. Having an office green team, led by a "Green Champion," has worked for dozens of companies that have impressive environmental performance. By organizing a green team that collectively represents each area of operations within your office, the workload can be distributed to the right individuals in each area, and you will have a good understanding of the challenges and opportunities that exist in each part of your business.

For time management, your green team could have a one-hour meeting every one to two months, and one short touch-base meeting (20 minutes) in between to check on progress and give brief updates. You can track progress using shared internal documents for quick correspondence and recording of data on key-performance indicators.

Going green is most successful when integrated slowly and deliberately into an organization, without completely distracting from your core purpose of operating, so give your program some structure and focus on small wins towards bigger goals.

1.1 We are already so busy!

If your main barrier to going green at your office is that you feel you are already too busy, try allocating a small and manageable amount of time to going green. To justify your time spent, focus on initiatives that will be time-savers in the long run. For example, changing your incandescent lightbulbs to LED bulbs will reduce the amount of time spent on changing lightbulbs because, on average, LEDs last more than ten times longer than incandescents.

Spending a small amount of time going green, even two hours per month, can go a long way to making for a healthier, leaner, and more efficient workplace.

1.2 Who would manage this?

Selecting a Green Champion: Some businesses get stuck trying to figure out who should be the force behind green activities. Ideally, the green champion will be someone in your business who is connected to all areas of your operations and understands the various facets of the organization. Often this person is a Chief Operating Office (COO), an administrative assistant, or an office manager. It is important that your green champion be someone not only well connected, but also respected amongst peers in the company. This individual will need to kindly persuade others to get on board with new initiatives, standards, and goals.

Building a Green Team: Each green team member should have a specific role and duty. This may be in a certain area of the business (e.g., washroom, print room) or targeted areas of environmental improvement (e.g., water, waste, electricity) in order to distribute the workload and assure that major areas have someone accountable for them. The green team should have direct lines of communication established with executives within the company in order to recommend changes that will require executive support or approval. If your office has multiple branches in different geographic areas, you can have small green teams at each office and arrange conference calls for the green team members to share challenges and new findings.

2. Barrier 2: Authority

2.1 We don't own the building

If your business is leasing space within a building, there may be several things that are not within your scope of authority to change. Hallway lighting, washroom facilities, parking areas, windows, and signage may be outside of your control. This is the case for many offices we have worked with, yet we have still found numerous green initiatives that can be taken in leased spaces. Things like purchasing, staff training, computer equipment, printing practices, and staff commuting are areas that most offices in leased spaces can tackle. In many cases, these are the areas that have the greatest environmental impact.

2.2 I don't know how to convince my boss

Perhaps your boss is not on board with becoming a green business yet. You may want to present the idea and show him or her how important it is for the business to start doing its part to protect the planet. You may be hesitant and feel like your boss will think this is a time-wasting, costly initiative that won't make a big difference to the company. However, we can assure you that it is not.

There are a variety of benefits that come with going green at your office and if you focus on the way that it will help solve a problem that your boss is focused on, bingo! He or she will be on board. Think as if you were in your boss' shoes. What would be the benefits for the business? Is it reducing costs, adding marketing value, improving community relations, complying with new regulations, reducing staff turnover, or simply being an awesome company? It is likely that one of these objectives is on the master list of things he or she is working on and you can use a green approach to help achieve them.

The lesson here is: Speak your boss' language and help him or her reach a broader goal in the company. If your boss cares about money, talk about the potential cost savings. If he or she cares about the brand, talk about how it can appeal to a wider range of consumers and increase your corporate profile. You get the point.

Let your boss know you have an idea of how this new initiative could work in the company. It will be a streamlined, timely, and cost-effective process. This book will help you organize a successful sustainability program in your office by engaging with your boss. Keep reading and take notes of the stages along the way to going green. This book is loaded with examples of simple actions that can have a big impact to get your company, and boss, on board and motivated to do more.

Example:

When I was 19, I worked at a coffee shop. I was taking environmental sciences and couldn't stand the wasted packaging, energy, and water that I saw at work. So, I started making efforts to green the shop. I put soft plastics and batteries under the counter and would later take them to the university to recycle. I made "turn lights off" signs in the washrooms and storage rooms and set up a small compost bin. It didn't take much for the owner to take notice.

"What the heck are you doing?" he asked.

Now, this wasn't the praise that I had been anticipating. He continued, "All this green stuff you are doing, it has to stop. I know you care about it, but I'm going to live another 40 years, what do I care?"

Shocked, I didn't know what to say. He was testing me, and rightly so. He was making sure I wasn't just exercising my own personal values in his shop. He wanted to see that I also had the best interest of the business in mind.

I took a breath, intimidated; and a sip of my cappuccino, buying time. He was scary, and ridiculously smart. Also, if I said something stupid he would probably give me a nickname that would last the extent of my job at the café. "OK," I said, "I'm doing this because I care, but I also believe this will be fantastic for business. For a few reasons; first: we waste a lot of energy and water here. I bet we could save 10 percent on our utility bills if we just smartened up — no investments in new equipment, just less waste. Second, I'm not the only "greenie" in this city, lots of people care about the environment. Just look at all the new green products in the grocery store. I'm pretty sure these giant companies have done their research on what people care about. If you are a green coffee shop, and show your values, you will not only have more loyal customers, but more loyal staff too. I bet people would want to work here just BECAUSE it is green. Furthermore, this is still new stuff. By being a green business, you can gain a marketing advantage and get free exposure for what you are doing. You could pull it right into the brand so when people think of this place they think of it being a green, awesome café where they love spending money."

I was breathless at that point, and he asked me to stop talking.

"OK, OK, maybe you have something here, but come up with a plan, tell me how it can be done ... "

This coffee shop went on to become a carbon-neutral establishment. We reduced our energy, water, and natural gas consumption. We took out one landfill bag of trash per week, instead of three or four per day. We started carrying eco-mugs, which were a hit. In the year following, staff turnover was cut in half. People stuck around longer because it was a cool, ethical place to work. And the customers? They loved it! So did the media. And my boss started giving talks on business sustainability, and taught other businesses how to go green.

Turns out, the tin man has a heart — especially if it is connected to his wallet.

3. Barrier 3: Cash

3.1 Going green is expensive

There is a general notion that everything green is more expensive. I blame our grocery stores for this. Buying the certified organic or green product is often more expensive because growing food in other countries with chemicals is cheaper than doing it without chemicals, it is as simple as that. But this "green premium" need not translate to your green office program. In fact, the opposite can be true — going green can be a major cost-reducer, having a positive impact on the bottom line. It can also build your marketability, customer loyalty, and staff morale, thereby influencing your top-line revenue.

To go green in your office, there should be a budget in place — something that is small and manageable for the company.

This money should be used for upgrades to the workplace, and should pay for changes that will save the business money immediately or within a reasonable payback time. When we work with a company to green their operations, the goal is to start with the low-hanging fruit and spend money in areas that will save them the most money. These savings can then be used to create a fund for future changes.

Example: By reducing paper consumption by 25 percent, a business can save hundreds of dollars every year — these savings can then be allocated toward the purchase of new lights that will save energy and costs. The cost savings in electricity can be allocated to a new, waste-free coffeemaker. The result of this series of transactions is a catalytic, cost-neutral program, fueled by its own savings.

The following chapters in this book will highlight ways for your office to save money and reduce your impact on the environment.

4. Barrier 4: Knowledge

Going green can be a confusing endeavor. While a great wealth of knowledge exists online, it can require hours of sifting through and is often completely overwhelming. When trying to determine the best solution for your office, you may find contradictory advice, an explosion of blogs, and more reports than you could ever find time to read.

This book is intended to give you both a practical guide and a strategy for greening your office. Whether you are a bike-riding, composting green keener, or new to the concept of a green business, we hope you will learn many valuable tips on how to reduce your environmental impact, save money, and enhance your brand. But hey, we don't know everything so here is a short list of our favorite resources for going green at the office:

- InHabitat.com
- David Suzuki Foundation (DavidSuzuki.org)
- Greenbiz.com
- SustainableBrands.com
- TreeHugger.com

There are also some fantastic industry associations, nonprofit groups, and online resources that your business can tap into to help you expand your horizon and learn more about business sustainability. Look into what is available in your area. Industry associations or nonprofit groups often offer a variety of learning opportunities such as the following:

- Webinars.
- Conferences.
- Seminars.
- Online Courses.
- Focus Groups.

5. Final Word on Barriers

Forty years ago, we didn't consider the environmental impact of our offices. Today, it is important for each and every business to do its part. While the barriers can seem insurmountable, a good strategy and small steps will make it come together. Incremental advances and a small amount of dedicated resources can have a positive impact on the planet and your business. You may look back a year from now and say, "Wow! Look how far we have come." That pride and corporate social responsibility will be well worth the effort.

4
What Are the Benefits of a Green Office?

The most common thing that can be gained through operating a green office is saving on the amount of products you purchase and the natural resources that you consume as a result of your day-to-day activities. Other benefits include boosting employee morale, gaining brand loyalty, and marketability, reducing your organization's risk in a changing world, creating meaningful and real engagement with clients, and becoming a leader in sustainability.

1. Running a More Cost-Effective Office

People often assume that a green office is going to be more expensive to run. In reality, there can be significant cost savings involved. Table 1 shows the top ten cost savings that will conserve cash and reduce your impact on the environment. Note, these savings will vary depending on the cost of energy in your city but in general these are great ways to save money, regardless of your location.

Table 1
Top Ten Green Office Cost Savers

Office Saving Action	How	Cost Savings
Conserve energy at workstations.	Get staff to turn off their computers and monitors at night or put them into sleep mode when not in use.	Can save up to 300 kWh a year or nearly $30 per desk. Imagine the savings throughout your entire office!
Switch to digital file storage.	Choose a cloud-based file storage system for your office and convert to digital storage.	Digital filing will save you time, money, and physical space with less printing, time spent shuffling papers, and areas needed for filing.
Get over bottled water.	Pledge to be a water-bottle-free office and ditch the water cooler. If your water quality is low, install a built-in filter for your tap.	Depending on the going rate for municipal water, the cost savings vary, but most utilities charge, less than a cent per liter for water. Compare that to $1+ per liter of bottled water.
Reduce energy usage from heating and cooling.	Assess your heating and cooling systems for opportunities to reduce energy usage such as insulation, programmable thermostats, turning the heat down a couple of degrees, or installing a more efficient boiler.	Cost savings from heating and cooling can be substantial. Upgrading an inefficient system can cut your fuel or electricity consumption in half. Small changes such as insulating bare copper piping and turning down the heat are low-cost options that will add up to significant savings.
Think before you buy new.	New office products are expensive. Wherever possible buy used and refurbished goods. Buying secondhand products keeps items out of the landfill and reduces the use of more raw materials.	Buying used office furniture can reduce your purchasing costs roughly in half.
Telecommute.	Telecommuting will save your staff time, energy, and money. Reducing the need to travel to work not only limits carbon emissions but will also reduce heating, lighting, and office equipment needs.	Offices have found they can reduce space requirements and utility costs by allowing employees to work from home on certain days. These costs vary by office.

Table 1 — Continued

Convert to LED lighting.	When your old lightbulbs burn out, replace them with LEDs. These products have an extended life span when compared to traditional lighting.	Although they will cost you more up front, you can save upwards of 50 percent on your energy costs for lighting, and LED bulbs can last up to ten years.
Print double-sided.	Printing on both sides of the paper can help save at least a quarter of your office paper.	Even in a small office, this can add up to hundreds of dollars in savings per year, depending on how much paper is used.
Rethink business travel.	Business travel can be a big time and money waster. You may not want to miss that first meeting with a new client but regular updates can be done virtually, online on FaceTime or Skype, or by phone.	Reducing your business travel by 25–50 percent can result in big cost savings. Many offices spend thousands on business travel every year. Assess the planned trip and decide which can be done virtually, or combined with other trips to reduce total travel costs.
Complete a waste audit.	Figuring out how much waste you generate will help you identify what products you are using too much of or where packaging materials are in excess.	Costs for product waste often fly under the radar in an office. An energy audit may find that you do not need to purchase certain items, or they can be replaced with a lower cost alternative.

2. Boosting Employee Morale

Going green can help boost employee morale as your team recognizes that the company they work for is taking ownership over its environmental and social impacts.

One business we worked with measured employee turnover before and after going green. After a year and a half of efforts to minimize its environmental impact and do more for the community, staff were sticking around longer and people with a higher level of education were applying to work there because of their environmental values.

Employee engagement is often a nebulous topic, but in this case, the dynamic is quite simple: Employees that are encouraged to take action in the workplace and share their ideas towards making the company better for the planet feel empowered and become more loyal to the company. Many studies suggest that employees are more likely to be satisfied with their workplace and their jobs when they are working for companies that are green because they feel the company is held to a higher level of integrity.

An additional benefit of being an environmental steward is that it offers a great opportunity to team build. A successful strategy for going green includes building upon employee ideas and enthusiasm by bringing them in to the decision-making process, which can help build valuable teamwork and team-building skills. Engaging employees in the decision-making process helps offices gain momentum and support as a result of the ideas that are being generated internally and from a cross section of employees instead of what may be considered a few "green keeners." In short, going green can give staff something to be proud of in their day-to-day activities while helping meet your organizational goals as an environmentally responsible office.

3. Brand Loyalty and Marketability

Green consumerism is on the rise with more people choosing to support brands and organizations that they trust and that align with their personal values and ethics. When we consider that more and more consumers are making decisions with their dollars in support of businesses that are taking care of the earth, it's clear to see why it is beneficial to start taking action now. Being an early adopter is also a great way to move your brand above other companies and gain a competitive advantage.

4. Reducing Risk in a Changing World

The future is wrought with uncertainty. Whether it is a changing climate, increasing energy costs, or a shift in consumer preferences, all can impact the success of your business. The reality is that we live in a world facing unprecedented change, but with these challenges comes tremendous opportunities. Finding ways in which your organization can take advantage of and prepare for these challenges will be key to sustaining your business and organization in the long term.

With finite resources and a growing global population, rising energy costs, carbon taxes, and increased environmental regulations have been forecasted as the reality of our near future. By reducing your dependence on energy and natural resources your business will also reduce exposure to the uncertainties of shifting prices and regulations related to the consumption of environmental resources.

5. Being a Leader in Office Sustainability

There are many forms of leadership when it comes to environmental sustainability. You may choose to be an ambassador, a supporter, or an innovator. Being an ambassador, you can help get the word out about certain environmental causes and help promote awareness in an attempt to foster stewardship. This may come from representing environmental interests on a board or committee, or encouraging innovation and leadership within your business sector.

As a supporter of environmental responsibility there are many different ways in which you can help local environmental organizations achieve their goals in areas that may fall outside of your typical sphere of influence. An example of this is having your business join an organization like 1% for the Planet. This organization has a mission to build, support, and activate an alliance of businesses that are financially committed to supporting nonprofit organizations that are working to create a healthy planet. 1% for the Planet businesses donate at least 1 percent of sales to nonprofit partners that are vetted based on their environmental stewardship and responsibility. To learn more about this initiative visit onepercentfortheplanet.org.

Although the definition of leadership can vary substantially depending on who you ask, we like the following definition: A process of social influence, which enlists the efforts of others towards the achievement of a common goal. Whether you are or want to become the leader is irrelevant. It may be that your role is to find the leadership figure within the organization that will help champion your green office initiative. Or you may lead by example and go about making meaningful changes within your office in order to help guide and direct others.

Regardless of your approach to green business leadership, all forms result in greater connectivity with the environmental community, setting a positive example for other businesses, and showcasing your values.

At this point, we have covered the basic framework for going green in the office and some of the barriers and benefits you may face along the way. Next, we will look at how to begin.

5
How to Get Started

For many individuals, it is easy to imagine all the things that could be done in their offices to go green yet hard to determine the best place to start. To build and maintain a cohesive sustainability program, we propose you use the following four phases to assess your impact, engage your team, implement changes, and market your results. Taking these steps will provide you with a clear path towards achieving your goals and becoming a green business.

1. The Four Phases of a Successful Green Office Program

There are four phases for implementing a successful green office program that will be covered in the following four sections.

1.1 Phase 1: Assessing your impact

When considering the environmental impact of your office there are some key areas that you are going to want to look at in order to determine where you stand. This is also known as developing a baseline assessment.

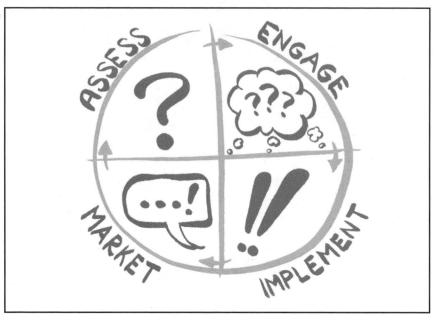

Figure 2: Four phases for a successful business sustainability program developed by Synergy Enterprises.

A baseline assessment will help you identify the current state of your operations in areas such as energy, water, paper, and transportation. You should visit all the areas of your office to identify any wasteful habits. Take some time to look at common behaviors (e.g., recycling habits, transportation, use of office equipment) and existing infrastructure (e.g., types of office equipment, office recycling streams, lighting, heating, purchased products), and determine some areas for potential action.

For an in-depth look at assessing your office, see Chapter 6.

1.2 Phase 2: Engage your team — internal and external stakeholders

After you have completed an assessment of your activities it is time to engage your team, both internal and external, on how to start taking action. Open up the conversation by shedding light on your current performance and areas where improvements could be made. Some will be quick wins and others may take considerably more time and investment. The important thing is to bring interested individuals into the conversation to start generating ideas on how you can collectively begin to make changes. You may be surprised at the great ideas that can come from having a green strategy session with your team.

Now that you have a better understanding of the actions you can take in your office, you may want to start looking towards your external team or clients for opportunities to improve your environmental performance.

In many companies, an environmental inititive is tasked to a single individual or a small group. To truly embrace a triple-bottom-line, everyone in your company should understand the big picture — the vision, goals, and the reason the company is going green — and how that big picture translates to their job and daily lives.

See Chapter 7 for more about engaging your team.

1.3 Phase 3: Implement your changes

Now that you have assessed your practices and engaged your team it is time to implement changes in your office. At this stage, you will want to develop an action plan, with approximate cost savings, assigned responsibilities, and timelines for each action. To make it manageable, you may want to stagger changes in the workplace over the course of multiple quarters. Make sure that everyone has access to the action plan, and that your business has a grasp of the resources that will be required and the benefits that will result from implementing your plan.

Depending on the types of changes that you are wanting to make, it may be as easy as buying new energy-efficient office equipment as part of a larger computer refresh that was scheduled to take place (this is where it pays to have representation from each department, such as IT and purchasing on your green team). You can measure the impact of these changes by calculating the average annual energy use for the old computers and compare that to the new computers, in order to estimate annual energy savings.

If you are looking to change behaviors in your office, plan a fun, engaging, and easy-to-measure environmental campaign.

This could include holding your First Annual Ugly Christmas Sweater Party, which coincides with an educational program about turning down your office's thermostats to save energy. Make a friendly competition out of it by giving out prizes for the ugliest sweaters, or to departments with the most participants.

See Chapter 8 for more concrete ways to green your office and measure results.

1.4 Phase 4: Market your performance

Now that you have gone through the first three phases of greening your office, it is time to start showcasing your successes. Having measured results of the changes made since your baseline assessment is powerful, and provides you with the opportunity to deliver facts and figures as a part of your messaging. You can include sustainability in your marketing through social media, website, promotional materials, and advertising campaigns.

Drawing sustainability into your brand will require more than an extra sentence here and there. You will need to look at how you present your brand and what key messages are true to your triple-bottom-line values and will appeal to your target audience. If you want to stand out as a green leader, it must become inherent in your brand and drawn into your core marketing and corporate identity.

One thing to be mindful of is to make sure that your claims are weighted with performance metrics that showcase real results. If you are not correctly measuring and reporting on the true environmental performance of your organization, then you could be seen as "greenwashing." Be sure that your marketing values are genuinely ingrained in the company and your actions and that you are backing up your results with real metrics and data.

See Chapter 10 for more about marketing your green initiatives.

6

How to Assess Your Office's Environmental Performance

When assessing your office's environmental performance you can break it down into a few distinct categories. These categories include the building your office is in, the water and energy consumed, the products your office purchases, how you move goods and services (including employee travel), and the waste you generate.

Your office can be designed, built, maintained, or retrofitted in a way that improves environmental performance. The most common way to assess your building's performance is to look at the previous years' electricity and utility bills to measure volumes of consumption and to consider the cost of these utilities on an annual basis. Determining these factors will not only help you create a baseline but they will also help you measure the potential benefit and cost savings of upgrades in your workplace.

To help guide your green office assessment we have provided you with Checklist 1 to see where you are already performing well and where you may be able to make some improvements. After the checklist you will find definitions for the terms that are in bold.

To assess your energy consumption, first identify a few key areas of energy usage. These include lighting, electronic equipment, and temperature controls, all of which are important to assess given that they will be in use during office hours and sometimes left on after closing.

For lighting, look at the types of lights that are installed in your office and determine if they are efficient or inefficient. Incandescent lighting may be the cheapest option, but they are not the most efficient and their useful life is much lower than newer technology such as CFL or LED. You may also want to look at the lights that are being used in your office space and figure out areas where unnecessary lights can be turned off or where lighting sensors could be installed. (You will find more information about lighting in Chapter 8, section **11**.)

Quick Tip: When trying to determine what type of bulbs are in your light fixtures, save yourself from tracking down a ladder that reaches your ceiling by asking your facility's management staff to show you which products they use to replace lights when they burn out.

The office equipment that you have in your building will likely include computers, monitors, laptops, printers, fax machines, and photocopiers. Determine if the equipment is turned off at night and look for labels such as ENERGY STAR on appliances and electronic equipment.

Another way to assess the efficiency of these items is to look at the energy-management settings on each device. They may still be set to the default settings which may not be efficient. Changing these settings can be easy and result in quick energy savings. All you need to do is go into your computer control panel and find the power-management settings. Alter the sleep settings so that you are making sure that you are not leaving these items on if they are being used infrequently or when you leave the office for a meeting.

In the average office, the heating, ventilation, and air conditioning (HVAC) system uses the largest portion of energy. As such,

Checklist 1
Green Office Assessment

Building and Operations

1. [ ] ( ) All nonemergency lights are turned off at night.
2. [ ] ( ) Computers and monitors set to sleep when not in use.
3. [ ] ( ) Motion sensors installed in less busy areas (e.g., washrooms, hallways, storage spaces) and/or "Lights Off" signage posted at light switches.
4. [ ] ( ) All thermostats set lower when space is unoccupied.
5. [ ] ( ) All sick stations have hand towels or *efficient hand dryers* in place of conventional dryers or paper towels.
6. [ ] ( ) Kitchen appliances are *ENERGY STAR®* certified.
7. [ ] ( ) Office equipment such as printers, fax machines, and photocopiers are *ENERGY STAR®* certified.
8. [ ] ( ) Lightbulbs are LED and all fluorescent tube lighting is T5 or T8.
9. [ ] ( ) Laptops and/or *ENERGY STAR®* or TCO-certified computers and monitors are used at workstations.
10. [ ] ( ) All hot water tanks and piping are insulated.
11. [ ] ( ) Windows are double-paned or draft-proofed and outdoor entrances and exits have been draft-sealed.
12. [ ] ( ) *Renewable Energy credits* are purchased for 100% of office electricity use.

Transportation

13. [ ] ( ) Bicycle parking provided for staff and clients.
14. [ ] ( ) Staff commute to work by bike, transit, carpooling, or walking.
15. [ ] ( ) Video or voice-conferencing technology is used to minimize traveling to/from meetings.
16. [ ] ( ) Local couriering/deliveries made by *low-* or *zero-emission transport* (e.g., bicycle, EV, hybrid, smart car).
17. [ ] ( ) Company-owned vehicles are *low-* or *zero-emission* models (e.g., bicycle, EV, hybrid, smart car).

Water

18. [ ] ( ) Tap water consumed rather than bottled water.
19. [ ] ( ) All faucets employ less than or equal to 6.0 liters per minute (1.6 gallons per minute) aerators.
20. [ ] ( ) All toilets are less than or equal to 6.0 liters per flush (1.6 gallons per flush) urinals are less than or equal to 1.9 liters per flush (0.5 gallons per flush).

Climate Action

21. [ ] ( ) Emissions are measured and, along with reduction plans and targets, are communicated to the staff and public.
22. [ ] ( ) All emissions are offset (including air travel) with verified carbon credits.

Purchasing and Products

23. [ ] ( ) No single-use products purchased for staff kitchen supplied (e.g., coffee cartridges, sugar packages, stir sticks).
24. [ ] ( ) Cleaning products are *eco-friendly*.
25. [ ] ( ) Select caterers that are actively committed to *sustainability*.
26. [ ] ( ) Office stationery supplies have more than or equal to 30% post-consumer recycled content.
27. [ ] ( ) Purchasing used office equipment, such as printers, photocopiers, and office furniture, instead of new products.

Waste

28. [ ] ( ) Reusable dishware is provided for staff use in place of disposable cups, plates, cutlery, etc.
29 [ ] ( ) All printers set to double-sided and/or both sides of paper is used before being recycled.
30. [ ] ( ) Paperless systems are in place (e.g., files are stored digitally, invoice, receipts, newsletters, memos delivered electronically).
31. [ ] ( ) All paper, cardboard, glass, tin, and rigid plastic are reused or recycled.
32. [ ] ( ) All food waste and soiled paper are composted.
33. [ ] ( ) All soft plastics (e.g., shrink-wrap, plastics bags) are recycled.
34. [ ] ( ) At least one other hard-to-recycle item is being recycled (e.g., foil-lined bags, Styrofoam™, lightbulbs, electronics, appliances).

Social

35. [   ] (   )   Employees are provided with clean, healthy, and safe working conditions, which are outlined in an employee manual.

36. [   ] (   )   Employees volunteer in a community event or charitable activity (at least one day per year).

37. [   ] (   )   Annual donations made to local environmental or community-related charities and nonprofits, at an amount of more than or equal to $50 per full-time employee.

38. [   ] (   )   Environmental sustainability is incorporated into the hiring process, employee orientations, and training.

39. [   ] (   )   Employees engage in pro bono services to the local community, environmental groups, nonprofit/charities, or others in need.

[ ]	=	Action implemented
( )	=	Action could easily be implemented
LED	=	Light Emitting Diode, high-efficient lightling
T5/T8	=	High-efficient models of Flourescent lighting
EV	=	Electric Vehicle
LpM	=	Liters per minute
LpF =		Liters per flush
(italics)	=	See definition below

Definitions

Eco-friendly Cleaners cause less harm to human health and the environment when compared to other competing products and services. Look for products that are biodegradable, pH balanced, EcoLogo™ Certified, Green Seal™ Certified, etc.

EcoLogo™ is an environmental standard and certification for products and services based in North America. EcoLogo™ provides assurance that products and services meet stringent environmental standards and are verified by a third-party auditor.

ENERGY STAR® is an international symbol that identifies products as the top-efficiency performer in their category. ENERGY STAR® is a government/industry partnership that makes it easy for businesses and consumers to save money and protect the environment.

Green Seal™ is an independent nonprofit organization dedicated to safeguarding the environment by promoting the manufacture, purchase, and use of environmentally responsible products and services. Green Seal™ ensures that products meet rigorous, science-based standards for human health and the environment.

High-Efficiency Hand Dryers use less energy than conventional dryers. VIGBC will consider Green Seal™ certified, ENERGY STAR® certified or equivalent as a high-efficiency hand dryer.

Kitchen Equipment includes fridges, freezers, ovens, and dishwashers. It will not include toasters, kettles, microwaves, or toaster ovens as they are not currently ENERGY STAR® rated.

Low-Emission Vehicle is a vehicle that has an average (city/highway) fuel-efficiency rating of 35 miles (56 km) per gallon or more.

Office Equipment includes fax machines, printers, multifunctional devices, televisions, and air purifiers or dehumidifiers.

Renewable Energy Credits recognize power companies that utilize environmentally friendly electricity generation (e.g., solar, wind, or bio-energy). Businesses can purchase these credits to reduce their environmental footprint and support green-energy generation.

Sustainable Caterers are those who take steps to reduce waste by limiting packaging and single-use items, using local, in-season food and Ocean Wise™ or Certified Organic products, and use low-carbon modes of transportation for their deliveries.

Verified Carbon Credits result from projects that have been verified for their role in reducing, avoiding, or sequestering carbon dioxide emissions or equivalent emissions such as methane gas. All carbon offset projects must meet certain standards and criteria and receive verification from a recognized independent third party.

it is important that your office space is not being overheated or overcooled, resulting in inflated energy bills. You can start to manage this by looking at the existing temperature settings on your thermostats and HVAC appliances. Ideal temperature settings will vary depending on your local climate but it is often best if during business hours the temperature is set no higher than 21 degrees Celsius or 71 degrees Fahrenheit, and turned down to 16 degrees Celsius or 61 degrees Fahrenheit when the office is vacant. These settings may not be appropriate during the coldest part of the winter, so be sure to speak with your facility's management staff about heating needs and make sure that an incident such as burst water pipes does not occur.

The most common products that are purchased by offices include paper, stationery, postage, and office equipment. Take an inventory of common products you purchase and determine if they are the most environmentally friendly choices, and if they are being purchased or used in excess. When assessing the products your office purchases you may also want to look at the total amount of money being spent. Once you have a better idea of the cost, you can identify opportunities to choose environmentally and socially responsible products and services.

Though it may seem removed from your core operations, parking, bike lock-up, and storage areas play an important role in supporting how staff get to and from work. One way to assess your office's transportation options is to look at the services that are provided to staff. Whether this is through the provision of parking stalls or bike lock-up areas, each can influence how people get to and from the office. As transportation is a major source of greenhouse gas (GHG) emissions and air pollution it is important to try and get people out of their vehicles and taking active modes of transportation (e.g., bicycling, walking, and transit). When you assess your building, look at the bike lock-up areas: Are they full every day? Is there a changing or shower area that can be used by staff and is it easily accessible and well-known? If not, it may be as easy as educating staff about these areas and how to access them.

To assess your waste, look for opportunities to divert waste entering the garbage into available recycling streams. What recycling streams are available may vary depending on the city you live in but it is always a good idea to call your city and ask them about what recycling services they offer and what additional recycling streams are offered by private companies (this may include soft plastic, foil-lined bags, organics, batteries). Conducting a waste audit may seem like a dirty task but it can be made easier with gloves, transparent garbage bags, and a scale. Using these three items, you can speak with your cleaning staff and have them leave behind a day's garbage (or week if you are ambitious) and weigh it to determine how much is going into a sanitary landfill, and then separate it into plastic bags based on locally available recycling streams. Then you can measure the amount of waste that still remains to determine how a recycling program could reduce the amount of waste your office generates.

Most offices use a considerable amount of water daily. The majority is used to flush toilets, to drink, and for washing dishes. This may not seem like much but every drop counts, as water scarcity and drought are becoming more common.

You may be able to track down your water bills and determine your annual or monthly consumption. If you are unable to get this information, it may be as easy as looking at the flow-rating labels on your toilets and faucets. If you can't find them on your toilets, they may be inside the reservoir (tank). A toilet that uses 6 liters or 1.6 gallons per flush is considered to be an efficient toilet. Anything more than this level is inefficient.

If you cannot find the flow rating on a faucet aerator, you can take a measuring device and put it under the tap and turn it on full blast for five seconds. Take the number of milliliters or ounces that were collected in those five seconds and multiply it by 12 to find out how many liters or gallons per minute the flow rating of the faucet is. Anything less than 6 liters or 1.6 gallons per minute is considered to be "low flow."

7
Engaging Your Team

We find employee engagement is often the missing link in corporate sustainability programs. It is more common to find a struggling, piecemeal program in which one passionate individual is responsible for 90 percent of the effort that goes into greening the office. Having one person do all the heavy lifting is convenient, but that person may soon burn out from the weight of shifting office culture. That is why engaging all employees in your sustainability program is crucial for cooperation and ensuring the long-term success of the program.

Engaged employees are defined as ones who fully understand and are enthusiastic about the purpose of the organization. To gain engagement from all employees, you will need a solid strategy and a framework for success including four cyclical components: Inspiration, Knowledge, Participation, and Celebration. (See Figure 3.)

1. *Seven Steps for Green Leadership and Transformation*

We find that effective green leadership takes shape in a process of change management. The following seven steps summarizes this process:

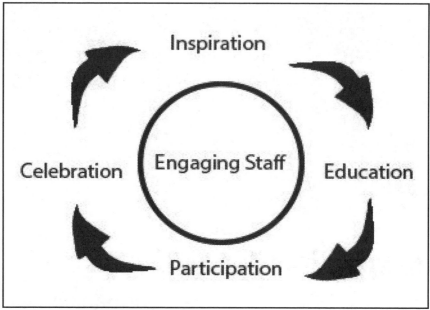

Figure 3: Four cyclical components for staff engagement in sustainability.

1. **Inspire change:** Send a clear message from the company's leadership on the future vision for the company and how sustainability will be incorporated and set the stage for engagement. Leadership needs to show that they are behind the initiative.

2. **Involve everyone:** Define how this high-level vision can be applied to your company. What are the values and initiatives that may transpire? This idea generation stage will get everyone involved and on board, since they had a part in creating what it will become.

3. **Create a timeline:** Change requires a continual, yet comfortable pace. Understand that you will not be able to change everything in the first quarter. Stage initiatives into phases for your company and tackle one at a time for smooth transitions. Allow your vision to slowly manifest and become ingrained into how the company operates.

4. **Rally a team:** Create a team that will put a dedicated effort towards going green. You may want to bring in external support or consultation in this phase to help guide your team.

5. **Communicate progress:** Those involved in step 2 should be informed of any new changes, actions, or challenges along the way. Something as simple as a quarterly progress report will keep people in touch and informed. Speak to the results so far, the wins, and make it fun! Include photos and charts. (Who doesn't love a good chart?)

6. **Celebrate the wins:** Remember where you started and how far you have come. Reflect on your baseline assessment. What has been acheived since then? Celebrate the efforts of your team and reward their efforts.

7. **Make it a cycle:** Remember that sustainability is a journey, not a destination. Have quarterly or annual brainstorming sessions, and think of new actions that can continually improve your performance. Celebrate along the way.

2. Inspiration

Inspiration is the fuel that makes great companies. When a team is inspired they inject positive and productive energy into the workplace, and can accomplish great things. It also enhances participation and engagement with current programs and policies.

To expect staff to comply with the new recycling program, printing protocols, and purchasing guidelines, they need to understand why these changes are taking place. This is where the big picture vision comes into play. Your company leadership should articulate why sustainability is important to the company, and present a vision for where the company is headed.

Following the Seven Steps for Green Leadership and Transformation, your team will have a better understanding of why these changes are happening, and you can expect more cooperation, excitement, and enthusiasm.

3. Communicating Changes in Corporate Culture

When the values of a company are communicated, set into action, and reinforced, they start to become part of its operational culture. Changing corporate culture is not without its challenges, but it will have great rewards. Infusing a general environmental awareness into your corporate culture can enhance engagement which can have positive spinoffs such as innovation, corporate pride, and employee happiness.

Stephen Whipp, Investment Advisor, Stephen Whipp Financial, a Division of Wolverton Securities, a green-certified office in Victoria, BC, said, "I find people working here with us are happier because of our environmental approach. They tell us that they are inspired by working in an office that they feel matches their values."

Sustainability offers a new lens through which to view your company and its stakeholders. High levels of employee engagement can lead to innovation and help companies find ways to improve the offerings of the company or new market niches to tap into. Companies with a strong sustainability culture can also become more attractive to top talent. There is a noticeable air of pride that comes with working in a green company. Furthering your positive impact, employees within your company will take these values to other places — their homes, future employers, and peers — we have seen this positive ripple effect in dozens of companies.

3.1 Quick tips for successful employee engagement

Here are a few tips to help you inspire and engage your employees.

- Share inspiring stories from other companies.
- Have internal ambassadors to keep departments on track.
- Reinforce that small changes result in big impacts over time.
- Set goals, share them, and make the results visible.
- Communicate how staff will benefit from going green.

3.2 Your environmental values and mission statement

A set of environmental values or a mission statement will anchor your sustainability program and guide its direction. Involve everyone in defining this for your company. Present your team with the opportunity to discuss this topic and include company leaders in this conversation to send a signal that sustainability is taken seriously. You may want to start with a brainstorming session and ask questions such as, "What core environmental values would you like to see at our company?" and, "How can we have a positive impact on our community?" Find the key themes in these answers and pull together an impactful statement or set of values that is true to your work and relevant to your company.

Example:

OUR VISION is a world in balance.

OUR MISSION is to engage our communities through inspiration, conservation and the provision of purposeful goods for exploring the natural world.

The CORE VALUES that guide everything we do:

Community

Sustainability

Integrity

Creativity

and

Adventure.

— Sitka Brand Vision, Mission and Core Values
(www.sitka.ca)

Fusing the sense of care and commitment to the environment into the fabric of your company will bring your team together with a new, additional purpose. While the result may be a simple mission statement, the conversation and inclusion of ideas will yield a stronger corporate culture of sustainability.

3.3 New hires

Incorporate green office principles and practices into hiring and employee orientation processes to immediately engage new hires. You may wish to include questions relating to environmental values and social well-being into the formal interview process to determine if the candidate will be a good fit with your vision for the company.

4. Form a Green Team

Employee-run green teams are formed to guide and implement green practices and policies at your office. Kicking off a green team is a great way to launch a sustainability program. While participation may be voluntary, it is ideal to have representation from the different areas of your business. This will give your green team a good understanding of how workplace changes will impact the different facets of your company. For example, if you have a small office, you may want one person from administration, one from project management, and one from marketing and communications. We suggest that a green team have a maximum size of six to eight people. If more would like to participate, break them into subgroups with specific topics like waste management, energy conservation, and green cleaning. Green teams may meet more frequently in the early stages (monthly) and less frequently at the later stages (quarterly). Support from the executive level of your company will be important for the green team to feel empowered and be successful.

5. Education and Awareness

We are fortunate to have incredible natural environments to enjoy and protect, but our office life can shelter us from these environments. Building a conscious culture in your office requires a general awareness of our natural environment and how your work may directly impact it.

Create educational opportunities for your staff on this topic. Webinars, seminars, TED Talks, green business associations, subscriptions, and conferences are examples of educational opportunities in which your team could partake. Your team should understand how your business operations create and impact the environment and what they can do about it. Building awareness and education will increase the knowledge base at your company with regards to green operations, cost-saving opportunities, and innovative products and services that can be used to reduce its environmental impact. At these events, your team members will connect with other peer businesses and learn from green leaders who are also working to create more responsible companies.

5.1 Create incentives

Rewarding environmental efforts can spur participation and positively reinforce healthy, environmental choices. Connect staff rewards to the progress achieved towards your environmental goals. For example, if your goal is to reduce energy consumption in your office by 25 percent, create an energy-saving incentive, such as a reward for the office, when that target is reached. Perhaps the reward is a new coffee machine for the office, a staff field trip, or gift certificates to local green businesses.

Another idea that worked great for a large office was offering a $20 gift certificate to each employee who ditched the trash bin at their desk. Staff could choose between a gift certificate for a local bike shop or smoothie bar.

If your goal is to get more staff biking, busing, or walking to work, you could offer free bus passes, or a reward for biking or walking a certain number of days throughout the month or year. At the Level Ground Trading office in Victoria, BC, employees sign onto their computers every morning and log how they got to work. Every two weeks staff receive their "green commute subsidy" with their paycheck. This subsidy is tied directly to how much distance they have chosen to ride, walk, carpool, and take the bus or subway during the pay period.

Don't forget the disincentives as well. Look at your company policies and ask yourself if you are encouraging unsustainable practices in any way. Do you offer free parking? Do you subsidize fuel costs for travel? Or do you incentivize less travel? Look at what kind of behaviors you may be fostering and how you can shift those to incent green practices.

5.2 Measure and communicate results

Choosing a few key performance indicators to measure success will help you clearly report on progress to everyone in the company. For example, you may choose to report on your waste diversion rate, energy usage, and paper consumption on a quarterly basis. We want to stress that reporting on progress in real numbers is a major motivator. You may be surprised how these results will keep people accountable to a shared goal. Be sure to set a target for where your company wants to be and show how close you are to reaching it. Send a brief memo or post the results somewhere visible for all staff to see.

5.3 Celebrate success

This step is often forgotten, and yet it is the most fun! Make sure to celebrate the wins, big or small. The sense of accomplishment along the way will keep your program moving forward. Throwing a BBQ with your favorite local foods and some great outdoor prizes is a great way to thank staff for their efforts while encouraging them to go and enjoy the outdoors.

8
Becoming a Green Office

1. *Paper and Printing*

There are many ways to find cost savings for your business and, as you can imagine, paper products can be expensive and generate large amounts of waste. We recognize that you may not become a completely paperless office (good luck trying to get by without Post-it Notes!), but there are many ways that you can use paper responsibly in your office.

To reduce the use of paper in your office we will touch on four basic areas for improvement: Rethink, Remodel, Repurpose, and Recycle.

1.1 *Rethink*

The first and most straightforward step to take is to rethink the ways that you use paper in your office. Think about paper in its raw form. There are all kinds of fancy coconut, sugar cane, and moon rock papers available now, but it is most likely that your paper originated from trees. How were these trees grown and harvested? Better yet, is the paper coming from recycled or post-consumer recycled paper products? Are you using too much paper? Can you reuse any paper products within the office?

Once we start to rethink how we use and waste paper in our offices, we can start to find ways to remodel processes, repurpose paper products, reduce the amount we use, and finally recycle the paper we do end up using.

Five Ways to Rethink Paper Use in the Office

1. Look at the types of paper you are purchasing. If you use less paper, you can pay for a paper product with recycled content at a similar cost and all you will have to do is change your purchasing habits. Asking your suppliers the following questions is an easy way to make this happen:

   • What is the recycled content of this paper?

   • How do you ship your products?

   • Is the paper Forest Stewardship Council (FSC) Certified?

2. Take a moment to talk to your staff about potential opportunities for saving paper. Generate ideas and assign responsibility for implementing them.

3. Consider changing an office process or activity to limit or eliminate your most paper-intensive practices. You may decide to create digital invoices, print all documents double sided, or start filing and storing documents digitally.

4. Move to a paperless editing system. Using track changes or other functions can be an effective and efficient way to draft, review, and finalize your documents. Programs such as Microsoft Word and OpenOffice Writer will let you put edits and comments into documents and help eliminate printing.

5. Encourage paperless meetings in your office. Send agendas electronically and use a projector or whiteboard to show the agenda and review documents with staff.

1.2 Remodel

Now that we have begun to rethink how we use paper in the office it is time to consider how we can remodel certain office processes in order to work towards a near paperless office. If you are looking to remodel a process, you may want to find out where you stand first by developing a baseline of your current paper use, then start to consider where you can gain efficiencies. A baseline for your paper consumption may come by working with the purchasers of your office paper and paper products to see how much paper and what types of paper you currently purchase. Your baseline should also determine how much money your office is spending on paper in order to build a business case for remodeling certain paper-intensive processes.

Once you have determined the baseline or total amount, type, and cost of paper used in your office it should be easy to find efficiencies. Here are a few key things to consider when remodeling office processes:

1. **File sharing:** There are many file-sharing services that can help you and your colleagues share internal documents and eliminate the need for printing.

2. **Paperless payments:** Start paying for your office bills online to reduce the amount of paper you use (e.g., checks, envelopes, stamps). This has the added advantage of reducing money spent on postage and envelopes not to mention the amount of time that staff will need to coordinate invoices, checks, and mail.

3. **Electronic document storage:** Storing documents can take up large amounts of space, paper, and run the risk of becoming damaged by fire or water. Filing office documents in an online platform or centralized server can help limit the amount of paper you print and also free up valuable office space.

4. **Electronic practices:** Most businesses still rely heavily on paper surveys, forms, and scanning of documents. These processes can be remodeled by using software that allows for electronic forms that the user can fill out and send electronically. This can eliminate the need to print, fill out, and scan documents saving time, money, and paper.

5. **Electronic invoices:** Sending your invoices digitally, via email can save paper, time, and money. At Synergy we saved 30 hours per month when we switched to electronic invoices. We also discovered our invoices are paid sooner because of this!

Case Study: Metrics Chartered Accountants

Metrics Chartered Accountants is a cloud-based accounting firm based out of Victoria, BC. This company is an innovator and leader in paperless office practices servicing clients across Canada; they help forward-thinking business owners take advantage of easy-to-use, online services. Everything is done using cloud-based online technology including uploading of receipts, conferencing services for meetings, and storage of records. Eliminating paper-based accounting while guaranteeing privacy and security to their clients is priority number one. This service is helping businesses save time and money while limiting the use of paper. Visit Metrics Chartered Accounting at www.getmetrics.ca to see how they are transforming business as usual through innovative approaches to paperless accounting.

1.3 Repurpose

Now that you have remodeled some of your office processes it is time to think about how you can give used paper a second life. Collect single-sided, nonconfidential paper and find ways to reuse it. This can be accomplished easily by providing trays for collecting nonconfidential office paper that has been used on one side. Whenever staff are done with a piece of paper that is single-sided they can deposit it in the tray and it can be used for other purposes.

Other purposes for single-sided paper include making notebooks, reusing for printing single-sided documents, or maybe using it for an art project! You can even reuse the backs of envelopes for making lists or taking quick notes at your desk, or relabeling file folders. Regardless of the way you choose, repurposing paper is the last step before you finally decide to send it off in style by recycling it.

1.4 Recycle

No matter where you are with your paper reduction efforts the first step you can take is to make sure that you are keeping paper out of the garbage, and ensure all paper products are being recycled. The amount of paper that ends up in the waste stream is still surprisingly high and most offices already pay for paper recycling as a part of their disposal services. If these are not a part of your current tenant agreement, it would be wise to talk to your landlord about having this included in the services he or she provides, or include it in the next round of lease negotiations.

The important thing about recycling paper, and any product for that matter, is to limit the amount of contamination that ends up in each recycling stream. What we mean by contamination is the inclusion of items that are not supposed to end up in the recycling stream (e.g., hard plastic in the paper collection bin). Many waste-hauling companies won't sort, so contaminated garbage could mean the whole lot is tossed into the garbage. No matter if you have all the bins in place for paper, hard and soft plastics, Styrofoam, organics, batteries, etc., this doesn't mean that your staff are going to sort them properly. Staff education is key; use prompts and graphics that show which items go in which bins. This will work wonders for getting staff to correctly sort their recycling.

We hope that you now have a better grasp on how you can reduce your paper consumption and make your office a nearly paperless one. Just remember — solutions to reducing printing will also result in significant cost savings and fewer trees harvested.

2. Office Products

We need many stationery products to run our office's; from staplers to file hangers and whiteboard markers, they all have an environmental impact. You may find you can do without some of these items. For items you need, it will be valuable to know how to identify credible environmental certifications that will tell you how these products were made.

Although your office is always going to need to purchase some office stationery, consider what items you actually need to have in order for your office to run smoothly and what items are simply unnecessary. Work with your suppliers to limit the amount of waste you generate by purchasing products that can be refilled instead of buying single-use versions of certain products. These include office pens, tape, markers, and other products that can be refilled or reused in the office instead of having to purchase new dispensers every time the cartridge runs out. This is going to save you money on the products you buy and greatly reduce the amount of waste your office generates. The best place to start is with your stationery supplier to make them aware of your desire to go green and seek alternatives that generate less waste.

FAST FACT: Approximately 10 percent of all landfill waste comes from office supplies. Many business owners have been making the switch to sustainable paper supplies but few consider the other office supplies that end up in the landfill. (BC Hydro Powersmart Program, 2014. https://www.bchydro.com/powersmart/business.html)

2.1 Questions to ask your stationery supplier

The first thing you want to do when looking to buy green products is to ask your stationery suppliers what green product alternatives they have available. Not sure what green products to ask for? The list in the environmental performance criteria section (see section **2.3**) will give you a better idea of what products to ask for and why they are preferable.

The first place to start is to ask your service providers what kind of criteria they use to label their products as being green. The most common approach to this is to use existing eco-labels or environmental certifications that are verified by a third party as meeting a set of criteria that are proven to have a reduced environmental impact or that use fewer natural resources in their manufacturing processes. A common example would be the use of post-consumer recycled content in paper or plastic products that are being sold by your stationery supply store.

Starting the conversation with your office suppliers will send a signal that green product choices are important to their customers and those that are committed to providing environmentally friendly products will have no trouble letting you know about the wide range of products that they stock and what environmental criteria they meet. With some stationery items, the greener alternative may come at a premium and you will have to make choices that fall within your allocated budget. Other items may have a greater lifetime and will warrant the extra few dollars because they will last longer than disposable or single-use items.

You can also ask your stationery providers if there are any green items that can be purchased in bulk for a discount. This may seem like it would have a small impact but it can help make the business case for going green while reducing transportation-related emissions as it will result in fewer deliveries and a lower carbon footprint.

Finally, ask your stationery providers what items can be returned to them for refilling, reuse, or responsible recycling. Some products now include the costs associated with the end-of-life processing and disposal with stationery providers handling returns for you.

In Canada, most of these waste-management services are provided by provincial and regional levels of government. As a result, the government works with product manufacturers to ensure appropriate steps are being taken to keep unnecessary items out of the landfill and connect individuals and businesses to local recycling solutions.

 An example of an initiative for connecting businesses and homeowners with local recycling services is through the Recycling Council of British Columbia. This nonprofit organization provides resources on retailer take-back programs and what they call the "Recyclepedia" which is a searchable database and smartphone app that provides you with the location of recycling services based on the item you are trying to recycle, specific type, and your location. Resources like these can help you limit your waste and connect you with office suppliers and organizations that take back certain products for responsible recycling.

2.2 Starting a green purchasing policy

"Early on, we created a purchasing checklist for anything we buy. This helps us adhere to our environmental values in daily purchasing decisions."

— Stephen Whipp, Investment Advisor,
Stephen Whipp Financial,
a Division of Wolverton Securities

A green purchasing policy may seem too formal for a small office, but it can be highly effective to put your purchasing guidelines in writing and ensure that people are following procedures that align with your principles as a green office. Be sure to develop a set of environmental and social preferable criteria for common products that are purchased in your office. It might be wise to complete a small inventory of the items that are purchased annually and start to envision what the costs would be to change these purchases into greener options. Start gradually with these initiatives and bring together your office green team to generate ideas on the best place to start with a green purchasing plan.

Once you have a draft of your plan you should seek approval from management to secure buy-in and support for the new policy. When the policy is in place it is important to consider how often it should be revised to reflect the changing nature of green office products and materials that are being used in your office. Look for products that meet your criteria (e.g., 30 percent post-consumer recycled content paper, metals, or plastics), can be refilled or re-used (e.g., toner), or avoid the use of more raw materials (e.g., staple-less stapler). Lastly, look to purchase products that have a recycling stream that is accessible and affordable for your office.

2.3 Environmental performance criteria

When looking to purchase green office products avoid those that make claims like "Natural" or "Green" and go with those that have had their performance tested by an independent third party. Table 2 shows a few key labels to look for.

Now that you have a better idea of some ways to green your office stationery products and an understanding of green product logos, you can ask your stationery supplier smart questions and develop a green purchasing guideline or policy.

Now we will explore how you can choose cleaning products to round out your green purchasing decisions.

3. Green Cleaning Products

Keeping our offices clean is important for aesthetics and general health, but some cleaning methods and products can have adverse effects on our health and the planet. Green cleaning is essential for a green office. Your employees will benefit from a healthier work environment and the planet will benefit from reduced packaging, toxicity, and resource extraction.

3.1 Environmental and health concerns

Did you know that many off-the-shelf cleaners contain muta-gens, carcinogens, and chemicals that can be devastating to water ecosystems? Many North American cities do not have water treatment facilities that adequately remove these chemicals; thus, they

Table 2
Green Labels

EcoLogo®	EcoLogo™	Sustainable product specifications that meet life-cycle based sustainability standards (e.g., raw material extraction, manufacturing, use, and disposal).
Green Seal®		Life-cycle based sustainability standards for products, services, and companies using third-party certification.
Forestry Stewardship Council®	FOREST STEWARDSHIP FSC COUNCIL	Certification of forestry operations to ensure that forestry practices are being audited for environmental performance and criteria.
Post-Consumer Recycled Content		Although there is no single certification agency for Post Consumer Recycled (PCR) content of products you will have to investigate these claims with your own due diligence, and look for the recycling symbol and the level of PCR that is noted on the product packaging.

are discharged into our waterways, harming fish and other aquatic life. To keep our rivers, oceans, and lakes clean we should make a conscious effort to purchase certified green cleaning products.

Where human health is concerned, commercial cleaning solutions can be harmful to the skin, irritate the eyes, and impact our respiratory systems. Green cleaning solutions can also reduce exposure to toxins and improve air quality. Knowing the potential damages caused by conventional cleaners, it is mind-boggling that we would consider using these chemicals in the places we live and work, especially when we spend so many hours of the day in them.

Another concern with cleaning products is the presence of Volatile Organic Compounds (VOCs). These molecules, found in many everyday cleaning products, become airborne and enter our skin and lungs. Many VOCs cause headaches, skin irritations, and dizziness. At high concentrations or long-term exposure, they may cause chronic diseases and cancer (more about VOCs in section **4.**).

If your business is concerned about the environment and the health of your workers (we assume you do because you are reading this book), here are the things to look for in a green cleaning product:

- Low or zero Volatile Organic Compounds (VOCs).
- Biodegradable.
- Nontoxic or low toxicity.
- No carcinogens, mutagens, or asthmagens.
- Non-petroleum based ingredients.
- Concentrated not diluted.
- Recycled content or recyclable packaging.
- Reduced transportation energy (local sourcing).
- No aerosol cans (chemicals can contaminate air).

> *"Cleaning products can present several health and environmental concerns. They may contain chemicals associated with eye, skin, or respiratory irritation, or other human health issues."*
>
> — Environmental Protection Agency

Here are some easy, do-it-yourself green cleaners:

1. **Window Cleaner:** Rather than an ammonium-based window cleaner, a 50:50 mix of water and vinegar will make your windows and mirrors shine. This is a cheaper solution and you can mix it yourself, reducing packaging waste. Add natural essential oils if you want a preferred scent.

2. **Hand soap:** Liquid castile soap can be found at health food stores and some drug stores. Pure, authentic castile soap is derived from vegetable oil (typically palm, coconut, jojoba, and olive). It is better for you and the environment because it is free of petrochemicals and chemical cleaning agents. Mix together 1/3 castile soap with 2/3 filtered water. Add essential oils if you like. Plant-derived natural oils such as Eucalyptus and Thieves Blend have natural antibacterial properties.

3. **Air freshener:** Good ol' baking soda! Put baking soda in a container that can ventilate and absorb odor. Refresh every three to five months. Add a few drops of essential oil to the soda for fragrance if you desire. You can compost the used baking soda.

3.2 Ten ingredients to avoid

1. Sodium lauryl sulphate (SLS) and sodium laureth sulphate (SLES) are common petroleum-based ingredients in cleaning products. These surfactants act as foaming agents. Environment Canada has categorized SLS as toxic to aquatic organisms; it is also a skin, eye, and respiratory tract irritant.

2. Phthalates can be found in fragranced household products. Often included in the ingredient "fragrance" or "parfum," phthalates are known endocrine disrupters, which impact the balance of hormones in the body.

3. Heavy metals such as hexavalent chromium, lead, or selenium.

4. Triclosan is an antibacterial agent that is found in hand sanitizers, antibacterial products, and even some toothpaste. There have been dangerous levels detected in some rivers, where triclosan can be toxic to water life. It is suspected to disrupt endocrine functions.

5. 2-Butoxyethanol is found in multipurpose cleaners. This ingredient has been linked to liver and kidney damage when inhaled. The healthier option is a surface or window cleaner with vinegar as the cleaning agent.

6. Ammonium is found in common glass cleaners; ammonium is a strong irritant and has been linked to asthma and chronic bronchitis.

7. Chlorinated phenols can be found in washroom cleaners such as toilet bowl cleaners. These phenols are toxic to respiratory and circulatory systems.

8. Diethylene glycol can be found in window cleaners and can have adverse effects on nervous systems.

9. Formaldehyde is found in many deodorizers. Formaldehyde is a respiratory irritant and suspected carcinogen.

10. Chlorine can be found in washroom and other heavy cleaners. Chlorine is a respiratory irritant when inhaled. A good alternative is baking soda-based natural cleaners, or vinegar and borax.

Search online for the Green Seal® Certified Cleaning Product list for many alternatives, or seek other natural options.

3.2a Synthetic fragrances

Synthetic fragrances, found in air fresheners and deodorizers, are a major health concern. Many off-the-shelf air fresheners contain carcinogens such as formaldehyde and other toxic substances including xylene, a known neurotoxin. "Fragrance" is often a listed ingredient in cleaning products; however, a fragrance may contain dozens of different chemicals. Don't be fooled by "fresh lilac" or "sea mist," some of these chemicals may be toxic and inflict asthma or other health issues. Going scent-free or choosing naturally derived scents is a healthier option. In fact, many offices are now instituting a "scent-free " policy to encourage workers to avoid using perfumes and synthetic fragrances before entering the office environment. This policy is especially beneficial for individuals who are sensitive to synthetic fragrances. Many offices can also make better use of ventilating with fans and deodorizing with baking soda instead of masking smells.

3.2b A word about hand sanitizers

Hand sanitizers, common in malls, doctor's offices, and in tiny bottles next to cashiers is an alcohol and triclosan-based liquid. It kills 99.9 percent of bacteria on your hands, but sanitization can be overkill. I'm not a doctor, but I do have a degree in biology, and if there is one thing I learned about, it's germs. Five years of germ science. I learned that while we are killing 99.9 percent of bacteria, there is the potential that 0.01 percent will mutate and survive sanitation; thus, we are killing the weak and allowing the superbugs to reproduce. These heavy handed sanitizers were traditionally used in areas where contamination has a high health risk. For the average person, this level of sanitation can be more than he or she needs. Common soap also kills bacteria and doesn't dry out the skin the way alcohol-based sanitizers can.

For germaphobes out there (you know who you are) the best solution is to limit use of hand sanitizers to high-risk areas where water and soap are not readily available.

3.3 Your janitorial service

Green cleaning companies make use of approved and certified green products in the form of mops, vacuums, soaps, and other energy-saving tools and equipment. Their staff of professionals have undergone training for green cleaning. Green cleaning services will typically include dusting of cabinets and shelves, vacuuming the carpets, sweeping and scrubbing floors, emptying and disinfecting the trash bins, and disinfecting doorknobs and telephone handsets.

Communicate with your cleaning/janitorial service about your preference for green products, and the health benefits for your employees. Give them a list of the types of cleaning products you would like them to avoid using, and a list of alternatives you would prefer, with specific environmental and safety certifications.

3.4 The greenest way to dry hands

Should we use paper towel or electric hand dryers? We get this question a lot. Many business managers are unsure of what the most cost-effective and environmentally friendly method is for hand drying. One option consumes paper, the other consumes electricity. What if you use recycled paper towel? What if your hand dryer is super-efficient? These are all important factors, but in general we find that hand dryers are the greener solution. Paper towel has a high carbon footprint, when you consider the energy, trees, and transportation fuel that goes into making and distributing paper towel and the waste that is generated once used. We recommend businesses choose electric hand dryers with a green certification such as ENERGY STAR.

In one particular business, we calculated their annual spending on paper towel. The total was $1,970. An efficient hand dryer costs $400 and would consume approximately $80 worth of electricity per year. The cost savings would be $1,490, making this a great investment. In fact, these new hand dryers would pay back in savings in less than three months! This is a common scenario in high-traffic washrooms. If you lease space and your building has shared washroom facilities, present this business case for efficient hand dryers to your property manager or building owner.

If you decide to use paper towel, you can at least recycle or compost this waste. In your washrooms, make sure there are two bins, one for paper towel and one for garbage. Be sure to place the paper towel bin directly below or beside the dispenser so that it is natural for people to toss wet towels into the correct bin. Have a bin for garbage near the door or toilet — this bin should be much smaller. It is important to label these bins very clearly as "Garbage only; no paper towel" and "Paper towel only." Your used paper towel can be disposed of through regular paper recycling or composted. Check with your waste-management provider to decide which option is best. Also, if you are still planning on using paper towel, ask for 100 percent post-consumer recycled content paper towel instead of virgin paper.

With hand dryers, be sure they are properly serviced. Otherwise, bacteria can build up in the air filters and, well, it might not be much cleaner than using someone else's paper towel.

As for toilet paper, you can hardly suggest that people use less toilet paper without getting strange looks, but it never hurts to have a reminder on the dispenser. You can order stickers that state "Remember … these come from trees!" from www.thesecomefromtrees.blogspot.ca. You may be surprised to learn that many types of toilet paper are made of post-consumer recycled materials. Be sure to ask for it the next time you are putting in your regular order.

3.5 Packaging and waste reduction

Plastic consumption globally is on the rise and cleaning products are a hefty contributor to the waste generated from them. Cleaning products sold in bulk, or concentrated forms, help to reduce packaging. Most Green Seal Certified cleaning products are sold in concentrated or ultra-concentrated form for reduced volume

Checklist 2
Assess Your Cleaning Products

	Window Cleaner	Dish Soap	Hand Soap	Sanitizer	Multipurpose Cleaner	Washroom Cleaner	Air Freshener
Is it green certified with a reputable logo?							
Does it contain synthetic frangrance?							
Does it contain toxic compounds?							
Does it come in refillable packaging?							
Is it in concentrated form, or have reduced packaging?							
Is the package recyclable?							
Is it made close to home (is it the most local option)?							

of product, which also reduces transportation emissions. (See Checklist 2.)

Refillable products, such as hand soap dispensers, can also reduce your packaging waste. A great example is foaming hand soap dispensers in washrooms. Many soap dispensers have cartridge systems with liquid soap inside a soft plastic bag, with a hard plastic and metal tip. These cartridges are difficult to recycle because of their many different components. A more economical and environmentally friendly solution are refillable foaming hand soap dispensers. To make the soap, simply dilute regular liquid hand soap in water (approximately a 3:1 ratio). With this simple solution, you can keep those cartridges out of landfills and reduce packaging by diluting your own liquid hand soap. You can do this in one-gallon containers for easy refilling. This may seem like ANOTHER step to going green, and it is, but it will pay off in cost and savings.

For reduced packaging, look for the following:

- Concentrated products.

- Recyclable packaging.
- Nonaerosol spray bottles, ideally ones that can be refilled.
- Refillable containers.
- Recycled-content packaging (look for post-consumer or recycled percentage).

4. Volatile Organic Compounds (VOCs) and Indoor Air Quality

In indoor environments our air can become toxic. This condition has been named the "sick building syndrome" or SBS, which causes building-related illnesses (Environmental Protection Agency. 1991. "Indoor Air Facts No. 4 Sick Building Syndrome"). Sick building syndrome occurs when a space is poorly ventilated and/or has high levels of air pollutants including Volatile Organic Compounds (VOCs).

In addition to cleaning products, items in your office that produce VOCs may include:

- Paint.
- Glues.
- Electronic equipment.
- New synthetic textiles.
- Carpet.
- Drywall.
- Furniture.

An easy way to improve air quality is having plants that will clean the air you breathe of harmful VOCs, such as formaldehyde, and increase the available oxygen. Here are a few examples of common indoor plants that actively absorb VOCs:

- English ivy.
- Spider plants.
- Golden pathos.

While greenery will add to your workplace and help enhance air quality, it is critical to assure that your ventilation system is performing properly and has clean filters. To gain a better understanding of your air quality, you can hire a professional service to assess your indoor air quality (IAQ) by measuring the ventilation rate and possible contaminant sources. If you find you have a low IAQ, identify the sources of air contaminants and relocate or remove them and look for ways to increase your ventilation. While indoor air quality might seem difficult to grasp, simple efforts to enhance the air your team is breathing can have a positive impact on their health and productivity. Take care of the air you breathe.

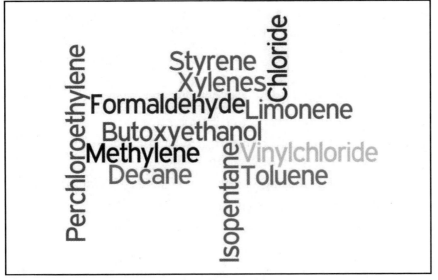

Figure 4: Common VOCs found in our offices and homes.

5. Catering and Food Products

5.1 Your coffee machine

If your business is like ours, this machine is perhaps the most important piece of equipment in the office. Without it, at least half of our staff members are "unable to work." I remember one day, we were out of caffeinated coffee, so I made a batch of decaf at 8:00 a.m. Closer to noon, our data technician, Zack, claimed he was "feeling funny" that day. When he discovered I made a batch of decaf, he was outraged. He stood in front my desk, "Why, why?! How could you do this to me?!" I would expect a similar reaction if I had put his paycheck in the shredder. Ah yes, coffee is a wonderful, delicious crutch. However, our love for coffee is not without an environmental impact.

A single cup of coffee takes approximately 37 gallons (or one bathtub) of water when you take into account the water required for growing the beans and processing them. Coffee growing regions are closer to the equator, with some of the top-growing regions including Central America, Africa, and South America. Thus, coffee must travel a long way to get to your office. Choosing a coffee supplier that sources directly from farmers and roasts locally can improve the freshness of your coffee, support local businesses, and reduce the emissions from transportation.

5.1a Considerations for a green coffee and tea station

- Low-waste coffee machines such as no-filter drip machines or French-press machines.
- Compost coffee grinds and tea bags.
- Use spoons instead of plastic or wooden stir sticks. If you do use wooden stir sticks, compost them.
- Have bulk sugar and cream (avoid single-serving packets).
- Choose local, organic sugar and cream products.
- Turn off machines at night and when not in use.

Buying green coffee and tea:

- Some of the major certifications offer third-party verified environmental standards practiced by the coffee grower and/ or roaster.
- Fair trade and organic certified coffee.
- Locally roasted coffee and local teas.
- Loose-leaf, low-waste tea and bulk coffee.
- Rainforest Alliance Certified: This certification promotes sustainable agricultural practices and fair treatment of workers. Certified coffees do not need to be organic.
- UTZ Certified: This certification emphasizes transparency within the supply chain and good agriculture practices that may preserve the habitat and ecosystem.
- Bird Friendly: A shade-grown certification developed by ecologists at the Smithsonian Migratory Bird Center. When coffee is shade grown, it is often higher quality and provides a habitat for birds and other species, making this an ecologically friendly way to grow coffee.

Note: While these certifications offer consumers confidence that the product is a more ethical choice, it is important to understand that although many small-scale farmers have ethical and sustainable practices, they cannot always afford certification. If your coffee provider has direct-trade relationships with farmers, you can ask what the best choice is for environmental sustainability and social well-being.

5.1b Single-serve coffee

This recent trend has caught the attention of many offices and many environmental groups. The amount of waste created by single-serving coffee machines (devices that brew single-serving pods, cups, or cartridges) is undeniable. The spent pod or cartridge is usually a combination of coffee, a foil lid, and plastic casing, making it difficult to find a way to recycle or compost the end product. In contrast, the waste from a French press machine is simply coffee grinds. A drip machine may use a paper filter and the waste (paper and coffee) is compostable.

This past year, I visited the office of a well-respected tech company. The owner breezed by their coffee station, "I feel guilt for having this single-serving coffee machine, but it's just so darn convenient." He was right. The cartridge removes the step for a person to have to figure out the right amount of grinds to put into a machine or press. Convenience has often trumped environmental choices (e.g., plastic shopping bags, paper coffee cups, and preportioned snacks). We can't avoid coming head on to a moralistic debate on this front: At what point do the incremental gains in convenience to our daily lives make it worth a mass creation of waste? With these ultra-convenient options, there is also a cost consideration. Single-serving coffee pods are typically 200 percent higher in price than regular coffee. We pay for convenience and so does the planet.

Case study: This past year, I was visiting the office of a large manufacturing company. As I meandered around their acres of property, they showed me many impressive things. The lighting was the latest, most efficient technology. They had a state-of-the-art pallet deconstruction machine. They were a group of techies and they had worked to make everything very efficient. We entered the lunch room and the fellow said, "We haven't really done much about this area yet." I opened the fridge and was blown away. Never have I seen so much plastic! The entire fridge was full of single-serving coffee cream containers, nothing else. There must have been a thousand of them. A wall of tiny plastic containers filled with small dollops of milk. Think of all the plastic waste that could be avoided by simply having a few gallon-sized jugs of milk! The engineers had tackled all the hard stuff, because they found LED photocell technology exciting (thank goodness for engineers). The creamers were overlooked; such a simple change that resulted in big cost and environmental savings.

5.2 Meeting supplies

If disposable dishware and cutlery is available or within sight, people will generally use it. Make sure your office cupboards are stocked with reusable dishware for staff use and meetings. To reduce your footprint (and cost) even further, purchase secondhand dishware. If you do choose to use disposable dishware and cutlery, you can look for green options that are recyclable and/or compostable. Some options are made with sugar cane, corn starch, palm leaves, bamboo, or uncoated paper.

Use dish towels that are washable instead of paper towels. If you do use paper towels, choose a sustainable option such as unbleached paper towel with 100 percent recycled or post-consumer content.

5.3 Catering

Choosing a green food and beverage service can reduce your waste, support local food providers, and reduce your carbon footprint. You can start by letting your catering company know that you are looking to source green products and services as a part of your overall sustainability program. (See Checklist 3.) The goal is to have a low-carbon catering service (low waste and local sourcing) and healthy menu options.

Asking this set of questions will help you determine how local catering companies size up in terms of sustainability.

By asking these questions, you will be sending a powerful signal to the catering company that going green is important to its customers (you). This is called supply-chain impact. Positive reinforcements like this can start a chain reaction and change the way that others do business. Hopefully, zero-waste catering services will be the norm someday soon. To get there, we have to let our service providers know what is important to us.

Checklist 3
Eight Questions to Ask Your Catering Company

1. Do you source local, seasonal, and organic produce?
2. Does your company recycle and compost all food waste?
3. Do you have reusable dishes (china, linen, etc.)?
4. Do you offer compostable cups, napkins, and cutlery?
5. Do you source eco-friendly meat and seafood (free range, organic, Oceanwise®)?
6. Can you supply juices and water in pitchers instead of individual cans or bottles?
7. Can you supply sugar, cream, jams, and other condiments in bowls or jars instead of single-serve packages?
8. Do you serve certified fair trade and organic coffee?

5.4 Growing food at the office

Having a small office garden will beautify your space and enhance your corporate culture of sustainability. I have seen many small offices grow pots of herbs in their lunchroom or food prep area. The herbs give the kitchen a fresh feel and offer a pleasant, mild aroma. These herbs can also be used to spruce up salads or other dishes.

In larger offices, sizable garden spaces can be cultivated on patios or in raised beds on the grounds near the office. One company had beans climbing up a south-facing wall, covering the bare cement with greenery and fresh vegetables.

Case Study: In Trail, BC, Canada, dozens of downtown businesses including a real estate agency, restaurant, insurance office, and firearms store grow veggies in planters near the street entrance. People are often surprised to see tomatoes, peppers, and trailing cucumber plants. The planter has a small sign in it that says, "Help yourself!" This is part of what is called Trail's incrEDIBLE Green Route, started by local business owners. Check out the project on Facebook at www.facebook.com/incredibletrail or at www. trailchamber.bc.ca/trails-incredible-green-route/.

It is important to make sure that you have a few staff to volunteer for the maintenance of the garden so that it doesn't get out of hand or neglected. If you do have a few willing volunteers, the garden can add a wonderful element to your office space and will connect your staff with how food is grown. Think about doing some light gardening at the office on your lunch break before taking some herbs and salad mix back to the kitchen to put together a quick salad. You can't get much more local and fresh than that.

If your local farmers have a food-box program, your office could support it by ordering a fresh box of fruits and/or veggies on a regular basis during the harvest season. This is a great way for employees to gain access to local, healthy snacks. Your business could sponsor this program as a treat for everyone, or employees who want to participate could pitch in a small amount of money every month and share the fresh produce.

6. Mail and Courier

When we first opened our office, I couldn't believe the amount of paper that came through our mail slot on a daily basis. In a week, it could be up to a ream of paper (a ream is 500 sheets). We were trying to limit our office-paper usage to ten reams per year, so the first things to go were the newsletters and flyers from our industry associations. Instead, we receive and send e-newsletters and event notices. You can reduce the amount of mail you receive by switching to digital subscriptions for newsletters, event invitations, flyers, and magazines you receive by mail. You can also sign up for the red-dot campaign which will put your office on a "non-flyer" and junk mail list. Look for the Red Dot Campaign online to sign up.

Simple actions such as reusing envelopes and boxes, using 100 percent post-consumer recycled envelopes, and printing on both sides of the paper will reduce the impact of your outgoing mail, but you can go even further by switching to paperless options.

When you add up the cost of the envelope, postage, paper, and time associated with mailing a document, mail and courier services can become a significant part of your expenses. It can also add to your environmental footprint from the use of paper and fuel for delivery. Green alternatives to mailing can reduce costs and your carbon footprint. They can also save on administration time. Assess the type of documents you mail on a regular basis, and make a list of alternatives.

A recent study by PitneyBowes, Inc. determined that the average carbon footprint of a single piece of mail is 20g of CO_2. But what about its grand alternative, the email? Mike Berners-Lee, author of *How Bad are Bananas? The Carbon Footprint of Everything,* has crunched the numbers and found that the carbon footprint of a regular email creates approximately 4g of CO_2. The problem is, we send more emails than ever, due to their supreme convenience. When you send an email, it draws on servers and computers, using power in ways that go unseen. While the option of digital communication has a lesser carbon footprint than mail, lean practices to reduce mass emailing within your office will save time, money, and carbon emissions. (See Table 3.)

Table 3
Green Alternatives to Mail

Mailed Goods	Green Alternative
Checks for stationery supplier.	Pay vendor online though e-transfer.
Signed internal documents.	Set up authorized electronic signature program and send PDF versions of signed documents.
Client invoices and receipts.	Email invoices and receipts to clients.
Thank-you gifts to clients.	Look for a green courier company.

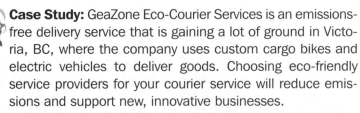

Case Study: GeaZone Eco-Courier Services is an emissions-free delivery service that is gaining a lot of ground in Victoria, BC, where the company uses custom cargo bikes and electric vehicles to deliver goods. Choosing eco-friendly service providers for your courier service will reduce emissions and support new, innovative businesses.

If you must ship goods, the method of shipping with the lowest carbon footprint per kilogram of weight is ocean freight, followed by ground transportation. Shipping by air is the method with the highest carbon footprint. If you have the option, chose the method with the lowest carbon footprint. It will often be the more affordable option as well.

7. Waste Management

Reducing your waste and improving your office recycling can be rewarding and impactful. Waste management affects everyone in the office and will require cooperation from your entire team to be successful.

"Working on reducing our garbage was what really got our team on board," recalled Dave Crothall, previous owner of a carbon neutral coffee shop, "We could all see the change and it motivated us to do more."

Although waste management is different depending on the region, county, or municipality you work in, the idea is to reduce your waste as much as possible and divert the rest to available recycling and composting facilities. Your efforts will result in less raw resources being extracted from the earth, visually less waste overall, and a proud team.

There are two key metrics for successfully managing your waste. First, you want to reduce the total, or absolute, volume of waste you are creating. Efforts by some offices to reduce waste have shown upwards of a 50 percent decrease in total waste by shifting purchases and improving office reuse practices. Second, your office should aim to increase your diversion rate from the landfill. With dedication, it is possible for your business to divert 95 percent of waste to appropriate recycling and composting services that exist in your area. Motivate your team by setting goals for these two metrics and communicate the results as your waste-management system and practices progress. (See Table 4.)

Table 4
Waste Reduction

Office ABC	Before	After	Result
Total Waste	100 kg/week	67 kg/week	33 percent reduction
Diversion Rate*	40 percent	75 percent	87.5 percent improvement

*Diversion rate is the total percentage of waste recycled or composted (i.e., diverted from landfill).

7.1 Conduct a waste audit

A waste audit is a report that details the type and quantity of waste generated at your office in a given week. We suggest conducting an initial waste audit to benchmark your performance and use as a comparison at a later date. When you have implemented some changes, you can conduct a second waste audit to see how your office has improved.

Once you understand what is going into each waste bin, you can determine where you need bins for organics and recycling. The total percentage of recycling versus organics and garbage will tell you what size each bin should be.

Your waste-management company, local municipality, or an environmental consulting firm may offer a more in-depth audit, which could determine the total weights and composition of each waste stream. More waste-management companies are weighing bins and keeping a record of the total weights per account. Contact your provider to find out what kind of information is available as it may help you complete your waste audit or measure your progress over time.

7.2 Your waste hauler

You will need to work with your local waste-management-service provider to optimize your system and include as many streams of recycling as possible. Find out what services are available to your business and what items it can recycle. If your main service provider cannot recycle all of the waste streams you create, you may need to use a combination of service providers that can take different types of waste and recycling. More services will result in more monthly costs, so it is important to make sure that you are reducing your volume of waste as much as possible.

Recycling streams to consider:

- Compost and organics.
- Paper and cardboard.
- Hard plastics.
- Metal.
- Glass.
- Soft plastics.
- Cartons and paper cups.
- Foil bags and wrappers.
- Styrofoam.
- Batteries.

- Ink toners and cartridges.
- Electronics.
- Lightbulbs.

Hard plastics are those numbered 1 through 7. If you are unsure, look for the number in the recycling symbol on the product. Soft plastics, such as bags and food wrap are more challenging to recycle. They are typically a lower grade product and can take more energy to recycle into a new product than rigid plastics. Wherever possible, it is best to avoid using excess soft plastics.

> "At Oughtred Coffee & Tea, we were able to drastically reduce waste at our offices by adding systems to recycle soft plastics, Styrofoam, electronics, foil bags, and compost organics. When we saw the amount of waste and where it was coming from, we also started changing the types of products we ordered for our offices."
>
> — John Oughtred, Oughtred Coffee & Tea

7.3 Organize your bin system

Green waste management requires good communication and a well-organized sorting system. It is very important to have visual, easy-to-read signage with as few words as possible. Ideally, a person should be able to glance at the sign and understand, in a split-second, what should go into that bin. Color-coded bins can help streamline your waste system and add another visual sorting cue (e.g., green for organics, black/gray for trash, and blue for recycling). Make sure to place bins at locations where the waste is created, to reduce the effort people have to make to dispose of something. A good rule of thumb is, if the trash bin is available, it will be used. Trash bins should be small and sparsely available, only in areas where waste is created that cannot be recycled or composted. For example, in your printing room, there is probably no need for a trash bin.

When we work with an office, one of the first things we do is remove all of the trash bins from individual desks and replace them with a small recycling bin. Most waste created at a workstation is recyclable. For trash, have a centrally located bin that clearly states that the bin is the last resort and for nonrecyclable items only. (See Checklist 4.)

Checklist 4
Waste Audit

Location: Print Room	Location:
Bin Size (L/Gal/m3): 10 gallons	Bin Size (L/Gal/m3):
Fill Frequency: Weekly	Fill Frequency:
Nonrecyclable Contents: • miscellaneous food wrappers Approximate percentage 10 %	Nonrecyclable Contents: Approximate percentage_____
Recyclable Contents: • paper • plastic Approximate percentage 80%	Recyclable Contents: Approximate percentage_____
Organic Contents: • Food: fruit peels Approximate percentage 10%	Organic Contents: Approximate percentage_____

In lunchrooms and at coffee stations, make sure an organics bin is available for disposal of food scraps, coffee grinds, and tea bags.

7.4 Composting at the office

The Environmental Protection Agency (EPA) has claimed that yard trimmings and food waste compose 23 percent of the total waste stream in the USA. Having an organics/composting bin will significantly reduce the amount of waste being sent to the trash.

Options for composting at your office will depend on your building type and the services available in your region. Many cities have private composting pick-up services available. Some composting services even pick up using bicycle-powered trailers.

Fruit flies and odor are two common concerns with composting. Remember, the same material was entering your trash bin, so there is not much difference between the compost and the waste you are creating. However, there are a few ways to mitigate odors and flies. First, a compost bin with a carbon filter built into the lid will help absorb odors. Make sure the bin is scheduled to be removed on a frequent basis (every one to three days, to avoid the sour smell that results from natural decomposition). To keep flies at bay, make sure your compost bin seals air tight when the lid is closed. Keeping fruit stored in a container or refrigerator instead of on counters will keep flies from reproducing (gross, I know, but they love to lay eggs in bananas).

For easy emptying, you may choose to use compostable bags in your bin. Make sure the bags are compostable and not just degradable, as degradable bags may still be made of plastic. Look for a bag that is made from cornstarch or another type of compostable, plant-based material.

7.5 Cost savings through waste management

By tackling waste management, your business can reduce operating costs in a few easy ways. First, reducing the amount of wasted product, such as stationery, reduces purchasing costs. Second, if your business can significantly reduce the average volume of waste it produces, you can reduce bin sizes or pick-up frequency by your waste-service provider, which will lower monthly service fees. Your business may also realize cost savings through sourcing refillable, repairable, and durable products that ultimately have a longer life span and alleviate the need to continually replace the same product or piece of equipment. (See Checklist 5.)

Checklist 5
Questions to Ask Your Recycling Provider

1. What items are accepted in the recycling streams you provide?
2. How should materials be sorted?
3. In your organics/compost stream, what items are not accepted?
4. For items that are not accepted in conventional recycling streams, are you aware of any alternative recycling options?
5. How and where are the waste streams processed and what new products do they become?

8. Transportation

When considering the environmental footprint of your office one thing that you may not think to look at is the way that staff get to and from work. In Canada, transportation emissions from personal-vehicle use accounted for 63 percent of total household emissions in 2005. With the majority of vehicle transportation emissions coming from individuals commuting to and from work, it is clear that office's can play a role in reducing the amount of greenhouse gases (GHGs) that are generated through daily travel. Although it may seem difficult to get people out of their single-occupancy vehicles and into more sustainable and lower carbon forms of commuting, there are many ways to do so while improving staff morale and boosting productivity.

This section will introduce you to the main ways in which you can support low-carbon commuting options for your office staff for daily travel and also for regular business travel. There are green commuting options and incentives that can be made available to staff which include: driver education, staff carpooling, subsidized bus passes, providing bicycling and walking facilities, and telecommuting. Consider how staff travel to work. There are many ways you can help lower the carbon footprint of your office by providing staff with access to electric vehicles, voice and video conferencing tools, bus passes, driver education, or by joining a car-share program.

8.1 Green commute: Driver education

How your staff get to work is probably beyond the control of your office, but you can provide staff with friendly tips and prompts or even conduct a workplace driver education challenge to encourage them to adopt green driving habits. You are probably wondering how you could possibly motivate staff to change their personal habits. Simple: It's all about the green — the money kind. Subtle changes can result in big savings over the course of a year of commuting to and from work.

1. **Drive smart.** Many factors affect the performance of your car but the most common mistakes are made from aggressive driving habits, speeding, and inefficient trip planning.

2. **Tune it up.** Getting regular maintenance can help your vehicle perform at maximum efficiency and maintain its value.

3. **Pump it up.** Making sure that your tires are pumped up to the proper level as noted in your owners' manual can save up to 3 percent on your fuel costs and extend the life of your tires.

4. **No idling.** Idling your vehicle can cost you a substantial amount of money over the year and have a negative impact

on air quality. Most modern cars only need a maximum of 30 seconds to warm up in the winter so encourage staff, wherever they go to go idle free.

5. **Give it a break.** Every now and then give your vehicle a break and take transit, carpool with a friend or colleague, or ride your bike to work.

8.2 Carpooling

One easy suggestion that may encourage staff to reduce the transportation emissions from their commute is to carpool to work with a coworker. To encourage this, provide preferential parking for staff who carpool to work. You will need to set out the specifics for accessing these spots (e.g., must have three or more people in the vehicle on arrival to work between the hours of 8:00 a.m. to 10:00 a.m.). Consider prime parking spots or at a lower cost, if parking fees apply.

Your company can also provide staff with resources to help coordinate carpooling. This could include an informal system on staff notice boards or through online surveys. You may also enroll your office in larger carpooling or Ride-Share programs. Simply type in your city name and "ride share" and there is likely to be a program that exists in your area. Be sure to encourage them to screen ride-share opportunities as you want to make sure that they are connecting to real people and are not giving out sensitive information.

An example from British Columbia is the Jack Bell Ride-Share program (www.online.ride-share.com/en/my/) which is a charitable organization that provides large scale public vanpooling services and exclusive online ride matching. More than 100 companies and organizations have joined this program and trust it to provide ride matching for their staff. This site has a database of ride-share opportunities for individuals throughout the province and you can join up with one of the Jack Bell Ride-Share fleet vehicles, be matched with someone using his or her own car, or offer others a ride using your own vehicle.

8.3 Guaranteed ride home

Sometimes the barrier for staff in commuting on public transit, by bicycle, walking, or carpooling is that they may need to get home in case of an emergency or personal illness. With this in mind, you can offer your staff a guaranteed ride home. This provides staff that commute to work using carpool, bicycle, walking, or public transit with a free and reliable ride home when an unexpected emergency arises. There may be an annual cap on the use of this service but it has been found to provide peace of mind knowing that they are able to go home if they are needed.

8.4 Subsidized bus passes

To encourage public transit use, your company could provide a subsidy for purchasing a monthly or an annual pass. This subsidy may be a percentage or a dollar amount off of the pass depending on the type. One way to make this quick and easy is to have staff sign up to have the reduced-bus-pass cost included in the form of easy payments in payroll deductions.

It may not seem like it will have a major impact but providing bus passes for business travel is a great way to get people engaged in active transportation — you do have to walk to and from the bus stops after all — and help reduce business travel emissions. All you will need to do is purchase a book of bus or transit tickets and place them at the front reception desk for use by staff. Make sure you have a sign-out sheet so that you can monitor the use of the program and how much travel by single-occupant vehicles is being avoided.

To strengthen support for a bus pass initiative, provide staff with education on available bus routes and times. It may take some time to get your team on board with this type of business travel but they may find it more relaxing to be driven to their morning meeting.

8.5 Bicycle and walking facilities

One barrier to staff traveling to work on foot or bicycle is the lack of adequate facilities available when they arrive. This includes bike lock-up areas, locker rooms, and shower facilities that your team can use to prepare for their work day after their journey to work. When considering bicycle lock-up and storage facilities, try to locate them in a covered area that is secure and easy to access for staff and visitors. Your company can support active transportation by providing incentives for achieving certain bicycling, walking, or public transit goals throughout the month or year. These incentives can be financial or related to their preferred method of green transportation (e.g., bike tune-ups, walking shoes, free bus pass, or gift certificate to a local bookstore).

Another way to encourage staff is through educational campaigns and training. These include bike training courses, access to cycling maps and trail routes, or bike facilities. A great resource for offices that want to encourage staff to walk and bicycle is the Victoria Transport Policy Institute which has a wealth of information on ways to encourage employees to adopt green transportation options (www.vtpi.org).

8.6 Telecommuting

If you are unfamiliar with the term telecommuting it refers to people who are able to work from home, as virtual employees, on a regular basis with the support of their office or management team. Although it may be difficult to imagine how anyone would be able to be as productive from home as they are at work there are many studies that show the personal, environmental, and cost benefits of working from home as little as once per week. Eliminating the need for individuals to commute to and from work is a great way to reduce the amount of travel emissions they generate while providing them with a better work-life balance, reducing stress, fuel costs, and commuting times.

If you live in a city with congestion and rush-hour traffic problems, this can be a great way to improve employee morale while helping foster trust and communication. The key here is to have a process in place for which employees are able to maintain their current level of service delivery while working from home. Some people (e.g., frontline administrative assistant) may simply not be able to get away with working from home on a regular basis whereas a data-entry clerk or a design technician may be able to work from home successfully and productively.

8.7 Green business travel: Electric vehicles

If your business owns or leases vehicles, you can reduce GHG emissions by changing your vehicles to more fuel-efficient models. Selecting a more fuel-efficient vehicle for business travel can help you save a substantial amount of money and help you tread lighter on the environment. You can find out how your vehicle compares to other models by going to fueleconomy.gov, which has an index of vehicle fuel-efficiency ratings for most that can be purchased in North America.

Over the past ten years, electric vehicles have become increasinly more popular, with major innovations coming from top brands. Although the cost of an electric vehicle may be greater at the point of sale than a similar car in its class, it can provide you with dramatic savings over the life of the vehicle. The only limitation here is that you may need to purchase and install charging equipment for your vehicle. However, this can also attract clients to your office and is a great way to show your commitment to protecting the environment.

8.8 Voice and video-conferencing

There are many voice and video-conferencing software programs available in the marketplace. Examples include, but are not limited to, United Communications Polycom UC Software, Google Hangouts, Skype, FaceTime, and many more which can be used from your desktop or mobile phone. Providing your staff with access to these, whether formal or informal programs, on your office's computers and in meeting room spaces is a great way to limit the need for business travel and be innovative as an employer. Since many of these programs are free, you could also save on long-distance phone calls and travel.

Here are a few key things to consider when participating in a video-conferencing program:

1. Maintain eye contact: Showing the other participants that you are paying attention.

2. Use your mute function: Be sure to utilize the mute function during large conference calls to ensure that the main speakers can be heard clearly and to limit noise interruptions.

3. Buy the right equipment to suit your needs: If you run voice and video conferences or meetings regularly, you are going to want to make sure that you are using good technology that limits service interruptions and is easy to use for others.

4. Provide staff with technical support: Providing staff with proper training and education on how to use these systems effectively is important and can make or break the success of these services.

8.9 Driver Education

If you are an office that has fleet vehicles, you may want to consider enrolling your frequent drivers in an efficient-driving course or education seminar. Conversely you may want to provide them with fuel-efficient driving tips that can help them be more eco-conscious drivers and also help save fuel. Luckily, there are many things that can help improve the fuel efficiency of your fleet such as those mentioned in section **8.1**.

8.10 Joining a car-share program

Joining a car-share program can reduce the need for your office staff to rely on vehicles and allow them to access a greater pool of vehicles that are available from private or not-for-profit organizations. For example, the Victoria Car Share Co-operative provides several different membership options depending on your expected frequency of use. Once you are a member, you will go through a brief orientation process so that you are aware of how the program works. Vehicles are booked online or by phone and can be booked in specific time increments (typically by the half hour). This example is a "round-trip" car-sharing service which means that you must return the car to the same location that you picked it up from. Other car-share programs such as Car2Go allow you to leave the car parked in any area within a predetermined boundary (i.e., does not need to be returned to the location from which you picked it up).

If you have staff that travel frequently, signing them up as members of a car-share program may be a great way to save you from having to purchase a vehicle. You may want to look into having a car-sharing vehicle dedicated to your office during office hours and then available to the public outside of traditional office hours. Either way this can be a fun way to get staff on the go and support a local alternative to private vehicle ownership.

9. Water

> "Water, water, everywhere, nor any drop to drink"
>
> — Samuel Taylor Coleridge,
> *The Rime of the Ancient Mariner*

Although this adage from 1798 may seem abstract, it sheds light on the growing problem of water scarcity that our communities face. Water is abundant, and yet, us humans have continually polluted and fouled our water supplies and altered them in ways that we are only starting to understand the true consequences. All direness aside, there are many ways in which your office can take steps to prevent water waste and pollution. This is especially important as the US Environmental Protection Agency estimates that office buildings consume approximately 9 percent of the total water used in commercial and institutional facilities in the US.

Similar to the cost of energy, the cost of water is anticipated to rise greatly over the next decade and with it will come more emphasis on the cost savings that can be achieved through water conservation.

9.1 Drinking water

The first place to start in the office is with the water you drink. Many offices pay hundreds if not thousands of dollars annually on bottled water that may be of equal or lesser quality than the water that is available out of the tap. True, there may be old pipes in your office which may be generating some specific water-quality issues but these can be overcome through the installation of an on-site filtration system that can remove debris and other unwanted chemicals such as chlorine and trihalomethanes (which results when chlorine reacts with organic matter in water). Many faucet-filtration systems are available on the market today. The important thing for you to consider is what elements you want to remove from your tap water to find the right product to get the job done.

Tap water is delivered to you in a manner that is typically far cheaper and results in fewer GHG emissions being released into the atmosphere. Whereas bottled water has often comes from far away sources and has high transportation emissions associated with delivery. Local bottled water suppliers will have lower travel miles but the water quality may be similar to your local or municipal water supply and at a substantially higher cost per liter or gallon. A quick cost comparison of water rates in Victoria, BC, shows the cost of 18.5 liters (4.9 gallons) of water supplied by the municipality to be 2.2 cents whereas the comparable amount from a local water supplier is $9.50 for 18.5 liters (4.9 gallons). Those numbers speak for themselves.

Another factor to consider is the energy costs associated with running a water cooler 24 hours a day, seven days a week. This can result in a considerable amount of energy consumption throughout the year and is an added cost that you may not be considering when examining the impact of purchasing bottled water.

9.2 Other water use in the office

Other common water users in the office are toilets and faucets which account for approximately 50 percent of office water use. Toilets are major users of water and old inefficient models can use 13 liters (3.4 gallons) of potable water every time the toilet is flushed. Although many building codes now mandate that any new toilet installations are low-flow models, considered to be 6 liters (1.6 gallons) per flush or less. Many buildings still use the old inefficient models. To help save water and money, consider replacing your old toilets with low-flow models. Many local governments want to encourage water conservation, often to reduce the need for costly water supply projects, and will provide rebates and incentives for the replacement of old inefficient toilets. Be sure to check your local government or water supplier's website to learn more about potential rebate programs and eligibility requirements.

Another quick way to save water in your office is to change the faucet aerators in your kitchens and bathrooms. In many cases faucets send too much water down the drain. Switching out your old faucet aerator can be quick and easy. Pick up a model that has a flow rating of 6 liters (1.6 gallons) per minute or less, and some t-tape for sealing your new faucet aerator in place. To install you may require a pipe wrench to remove the old faucet and to secure the new faucet in place. You will want to wrap the threaded part of the faucet aerator with t-tape before threading it into place. Most often you can seal the faucet aerator with just your hands but if it shows any sign of leaks, use the pipe wrench to secure the aerator in place.

9.3 Landscaping

The final area that your office may use water is outdoors to water plants and grass. Although this may not seem like a large amount of water it is approximately 22 percent of office water use. You should consider designing water efficient landscapes that take advantage of native plants that are drought tolerant or suitable for the local climate. This will help reduce the amount of outdoor watering that is needed and provide a landscape that matches the natural area of your region. Also, if you use irrigation systems, be sure to hire a professional landscape irrigation technician to install a water efficient system and ensure that it is being run and maintained properly. Lastly, irrigation controllers will help you water your landscape at times that limit water loss from evaporation (during the warmest times of the day) and a rain sensor can also make sure that you are not overwatering your landscape on rainy days.

10. Electronics

In today's office environment, electronics play a vital role. It is hard to imagine running a company without the ability to send a file immediately or use a computer program. We transport information at incredible rates and this had made companies faster and more dynamic with the ability to reach global markets while sipping a local espresso and chatting with coworkers. In their origin, electronics played a supplementary role to our paper-based, in-person business operations. Now, electronics have transformed our offices and this global revolution has increased our demand for energy. To meet these demands, hydroelectric dams, nuclear plants, and coal-fired generators are being built at alarming rates.

The International Energy Agency has estimated that about a third of global energy use is attributed to buildings. In an office, that power is sucked up by copy machines, computer screens, faxes, scanners, projectors, lighting, coffeemakers, and other items that have become work essentials.

Needless to say, saving energy is a big step towards greening your office and cutting your costs. Energy-smart offices are able to do the same work with less energy. This includes buying green electronics, using them wisely, and disposing of them responsibly. Read further to start reducing your energy consumption, costs, and impact on the planet.

10.1 Manage your power use

There are effective ways to monitor your power use without big investments. In working with various offices, we have found that simple behavioral changes in the office can reduce energy consumption anywhere between 5 to 20 percent. First, gain a solid understanding of the energy you consume. How many kilowatt hours per month is your average? What causes your energy usage to spike? Where is energy wasted and how can those energy leaks be eliminated? Answering these questions can make a big dent in your energy consumption.

An energy audit can help you understand how energy is being used in your office. You may be surprised at where your large energy consumers are. An audit will break down the energy consumed by the lights, equipment, heating and ventilation system, and other components in your office. Audits will often identify key areas for energy savings and will calculate the potential cost savings. Contact your utility company or a local environmental firm to get a cost estimate for an energy audit. Some utilities and local governments will have free energy audit programs available to businesses.

To conduct your own energy audit, you can use the following simplified format in Checklist 6.

Checklist 6
Energy Audit

Equipment Type	Wattage (W)	Quantity	Monthly Operating Hours	Monthly Power Usage
Printers	400 Watts	5	40	80,000 Watts
Ways to Reduce Energy: • Turn off printers at night to reduce standby power usage. • Use printers less; this will also conserve paper. • Reduce to three or four printers instead of five (as an example). • Begin replacing printers with more efficient models.				
Computers	300 Watts	20	160	960,000 Watts
Ways to Reduce Energy: • Turn off computers when not in use, even for ten minutes. • Replace monitors with high-efficient LCD alternatives. • Replace some desktop computers with laptop models. • Use power-saving modes to reduce energy consumption of each computer.				

Some things you can do:

1. **Install an energy monitor:** If you do not have an energy meter on your building that you can read, or if you would prefer to see your consumption in real time, an energy

monitor is a valuable device. Models are available for less than $250 and are simple for an electrician to install. If the meter is installed somewhere visible to staff, your office will be able to manage energy by noticing spikes in consumption, or the additional draw when a certain appliance is turned on. You can also detect phantom loads by looking at energy consumption when the office is inactive.

Using the meter, you can set goals for energy consumption and see the results when you buy green equipment or start new energy-efficient practices.

2. **Computer settings:** Resourcenation.com determined that the majority of energy usage by your computer happens when you are not sitting in front of it, but you can change that. Your computer's power-management settings can be altered to reduce energy consumed when the computer is not in use. Make it an office policy that all monitors are set to go into sleep mode after 15 minutes of inactivity and computers set to go into sleep mode after 30 minutes. Also make sure all computers are turned off at night and when someone is away from his or her desk for more than an hour. This is a zero-cost initiative that can make a big impact on your energy consumption.

3. **Timed power bars:** You can use timed power bars to automatically turn on and off electronics at set times of the day. This can be great for making sure workstations are powered up in the morning and completely shut down when people leave. They can also be used to manage night draws from kitchen appliances such as coffeemakers and microwaves that do not need to be left on standby during the evenings.

4. **Phantom loads:** These are a type of energy consumption that go unnoticed. They occur when devices such as stereos, phone chargers, and fax machines draw power when they are plugged in but not in use. This energy is completely wasted, for no gain. Most devices with a digital display draw phantom loads. To reduce your phantom loads, make sure equipment is turned off at night and over the weekend. Chargers for cell phones, batteries, and laptops also draw large phantom loads and will need to be unplugged when not in use to eliminate wasted energy.

Use this list to locate sources of phantom loads:

- Printer.
- Copy machine.
- Fax machine.
- Phone with display.
- Coffee machine with display.
- Stereo system.
- Microwave.
- Scanner.
- Mailing machine.
- Laptop chargers.
- Cell phone chargers.
- Battery chargers.
- Other: _____.
- Other: _____.

10.2 Choose energy-efficient devices

Your purchasing decisions for electronic devices can make a big difference to your total energy consumption. Buying energy-efficient devices can save you upwards of 40 percent, but you may wish to buy greener equipment as you need it instead of replacing still functioning computers. Consider an office-purchasing policy that states all new electronics purchased must be ENERGY STAR or equivalent.

ENERGY STAR is an international standard for energy-efficiency that originated in the USA in 1992. When a device has this certification, it often consumes 20 to 40 percent less energy than a conventional product of that type. Many large manufacturers have partnered with energy-standard companies to combat excessive energy use. You can find the ENERGY STAR label on lightbulbs, fridges, computers, heating systems, printers, fax machines, and more.

TCO Certification is an international third-party certification based out of Sweden. TCO helps offices make more environmentally and socially responsible IT product choices. This label can be found on IT-system components that have been designed and manufactured for environmental and social sustainability. This certification takes into consideration the whole product life cycle. Your office can look for the TCO certification on projectors, tablets, notebooks, displays, headsets, and more.

Globally, there are dozens of other green electronic certifications available. Other common international standards include ECO LOGO and EPE. Check out www.ecolabelindex.com if you are unsure of how one eco label compares to another.

10.2a Printers and copy machines

Printers and copy machines are often the most energy-intensive devices in the workplace. Printing less can result in reduced energy costs, and help you tread a little lighter on the planet. While there are some examples of paperless offices, most offices still do some printing.

If you are buying a new device or replacing a current system, it is important to know which option is the best for your wallet and the planet. ENERGY STAR certified high-speed copy machines can be up to 60 percent more energy efficient than noncertified models. They produce less greenhouse gases, consume less energy, and generate less heat. Overall, these are a more environmentally friendly choice and can result in major energy cost savings.

For smaller printers, a standard inkjet model consumes approximately 5 watts on standby mode and 50 watts while printing. Larger commercial printers consume more power, approximately 40 watts on standby and 400 watts while printing. An alternative to an inkjet printer is a laser model, which uses toner instead of ink; however, they consume more power than an inkjet. Recently, we looked at two comparable models and found that the inkjet printer used 120 watts and the laser printer used 350 watts, but the toner in a laser printer can last far longer than ink cartridges in an inkjet printer. Like most choices, it depends on your application and printing needs. Table 5 is a summary of the pros and cons of inkjet versus laser printers.

Many printers have the ability to print double-sided. Most new machines will allow you to change the default settings on your printer to do double-sided printing automatically, instead of relying on employees to manually select double-sided when they print each job. This simple change can save hundreds of dollars' worth of paper every year, even in small offices.

Table 5
Inkjet versus Laser Printers

Inkjet		Laser	
Pros	**Cons**	**Pros**	**Cons**
• Lower purchase cost. • Can print onto may kinds of paper. • Ink cartridges can be refilled.	• Ink refills are pricey. • Slower printing.	• Faster printing. • Toner cartridges last far longer than ink, making toner cheaper. • Toner cartridges can be refilled.	• Higher upfront costs to achieve savings in the long run.

10.2b Soy-based inks

Soy-based alternative inks produce less VOCs and are made of renewable resources, rather than petroleum. Ask your ink provider about the availability and cost of renewable inks such as soy and other plant-based alternatives.

10.2c Summary of green printing practices

- Actively reduce the amount of printing.
- Use both sides of paper, and set printer to default to double-sided printing.
- Choose a responsible paper, with a high-recycled content.
- Reduce margins and choose smaller font to reduce printing.
- Turn off printer at night.
- Use draft mode when possible to save on ink or toner.
- Purchase an energy-efficient printer.
- Purchase refillable ink or toner cartridges.
- Recycle printer and cartridges at the end of their life.

Remember: Printing uses energy and trees. Less paper is better, and if you do use paper, make an environmentally friendly choice.

10.2d Battery-powered devices

If you have any electronics in your office that use batteries, it is smart to make the investment in rechargeable batteries. While they are more expensive than single-use batteries, they will result in cost savings over the long term and less chemicals and metals being disposed of on a regular basis. For dead batteries, look for recycling options such as the Call2Recycle Program which will pay for you to send in a box of batteries that you have collected in your office. There are also more and more local businesses that sell these products and collect spent batteries for recycling.

10.2e Monitors

Cathode Ray Tube (CRT) monitors use more energy than Liquid Crystal Display (LCD) models. Many companies have ceased production of CRT monitors due to their high-energy demand. CRTs are also bulky, heavy, and generate excess heat. The main advantage of a CRT is the color-rendering ability, which is why they are still used in some graphic design offices. For most offices, LCDs are more common as they are the more energy-efficient choice. When looking to purchase a new monitor be sure to select one that has a green certification, such as ENERGY STAR or TCO Certified.

10.2f Laptops versus desktops

A laptop can use 50 percent less energy than a desktop. When it comes to energy efficiency, laptops win by a mile. To make a laptop more ergonomically suitable for working at a desk, you can place it on a riser and have an additional keyboard attached at a lower level.

10.2g Refurbishing electronics

Electronics such as computers have embedded energy in the components that they are comprised of. If you can get a computer custom built from recycled parts, or repair your existing computer, you will be helping to reduce the environmental impacts associated with computer manufacturing, the use of raw natural resources, and the disposal of old electronics.

Knowing a great computer builder has been a fantastic asset to our company. Because we were aiming to have a model green office, we have had some of our computers rebuilt, and we have purchased others that are new to us, but made of recycled parts. These have lasted as long as our brand new computers, and the great thing is, we know someone who can fix them.

10.2h Scanners and fax machines

Consider combining systems into one machine instead of having a copy machine, fax, printer, and scanner. These consolidated systems consume less power than having a machine for each of these functions. New combined systems are also incredibly efficient and have energy-management settings that can put them into sleep mode automatically after five to ten minutes without use.

10.2i Servers (a.k.a., energy gluttons)

There are two main types of server systems: physical and virtual. Both have the same functions, operating your email, file storage, printing systems, etc. Physical server systems have been found to operate at a low utilization, resulting in a relatively low efficiency of the overall system. A virtual server is a type of system that can optimize workloads and achieve greater energy efficiency. It also reduces waste heat. We have found that many businesses have server rooms with air conditioners. This counter-cooling results in additional wasted energy.

Your company will incur virtual server software and service costs, but these are quickly offset by the energy savings. Decommissioning excess servers can also result in big cost savings. With fewer systems, you will have the added benefit of less annual maintenance costs and more free space in your office.

With the great savings associated with server virtualization, some utility companies may offer rebates to help subsidize the process to switch to a virtual server system.

You can also look for servers with the ENERGY STAR mark. These servers use approximately 30 percent less energy, according to EPA estimates.

10.3 Dispose of electronics responsibly

Electronic waste is a growing global issue. With the average life span of cell phones, laptops, and other electronics being under five years, landfills are collecting tons of electronic waste. Leaching toxic chemicals and heavy metals, e-waste can damage water systems and the local environment. To reduce the e-waste created by your office, purchase durable goods and repair when you can. When your electronic device is completely toasted, there are recycling programs available to make sure your device does not end up in the landfill.

In Canada, you can donate old computers to the Computers for Schools program. Over the past decade, many states in the US have developed legislative acts and programs for electronic device take-back and responsible recycling. In Canada, many different electronic recycling programs exist.

11. Lighting

Lighting can account for up to 40 percent of electricity consumption in an office space. Globally, lighting accounts for 19 percent of electricity use. There are many ways to reduce energy consumption from lighting and reduce your operational costs. About 70 percent of office lighting uses are outdated, inefficient systems. New lighting technologies offer highly efficient models that consume a fraction of the energy that old models used. Before you go buying the latest and most expensive technology, it is important to assess the actual lighting needs of your office and strategically orientate and control lighting areas to minimize wasted energy.

Ways to Reduce Energy:

- Maximize natural light.
- Install motion sensors.
- Reduce lighting hours.
- Turn lights off at night.
- Utilize task lighting.
- Reduce total number of fixtures.
- Switch to efficient light fixtures.
- Switch to efficient lightbulbs.

11.1 Conduct a lighting audit

You can identify your major electricity draws by completing a lighting audit. This will help you find the best ways to reduce energy. We call this audit the "deep dive" because it measures the energy usage of every space within your office. Changing your lighting should reduce your energy consumption and your operating costs. Quantifying the savings of each lighting alternative can help your business make smart decisions for upgrades and focus on the areas that will make the biggest impact. (See Table 6.)

Table 6
Lighting Audit

	Area	Fixture Type	# of bulbs	Watts per bulb	Total Wattage	Operating hours	kWh in space
CURRENT	Kitchen	Flourescent T12 bulbs	24	60	1,440	12 hrs/day	17.28
ALTERNATIVE	Kitchen	Flourescent T8 bulbs	24	15	360	8 hrs/day (reduced hrs)	2.88

Calculating Your Savings:
kWh x Your Electricity Rate ($/kWh) = total daily cost
Example:
CURRENT:
17.28 kWh x $0.15/kWh = $2.59 per day
$2.59 per day x 365 days (open per year) = **$945 per year**

ALTERNATIVE:
2.88 kWh x $0.15/kWh = $0.43 per day
$0.43 per day x 365 days (open per year) = **$157 per year**
Total Savings for Lighting Change: $788 per year

11.2 Task lighting versus overhead lighting

The vast majority of office spaces have moved towards overhead fluorescent tube fixtures as the dominant source of light. These fixtures are cheap to install, but they may be inefficient and produce a poor quality of light. If you cannot change these fixtures immediately, make use of task lighting such as desk lamps (with LED or CFL bulbs), instead of relying on fluorescent lights. This can reduce energy load by providing targeted lighting to work areas. In our office, we find that task lighting with shades provides a warmer light, improving the ambiance of our workspace and setting a calm mood.

11.3 Maximizing natural light

The greenest light source is passive lighting from the sun. Daylight has additional health benefits for workers with reports of increased productivity and reduced stress. An effort to bring more daylight into your office will pay for itself by helping to create a better work environment. Consider daylight blinds which allow natural light to penetrate into office areas while maintaining privacy.

In some office arrangements, rooms with outdoor windows may block natural light from central office areas. Installing windows in the walls of the windowed offices will allow daylight to pass through to central areas and improve the amount of natural light that is available.

11.4 Turn off lights when spaces are empty

It still amazes us how many offices leave lights on overnight. Look at a cityscape at 3:00 a.m. It is not unusual to see 10 to 20 percent of all office towers still lit up and we can assume only a tiny fraction of these are due to night-owl workers. Changing policies and integrating sustainable practices into staff orientation can help make sure that the last person to leave turns out the lights. Reminders are helpful when we are busy buzzing around our offices.

Also make sure employees turn off lights when a space is not in use, such as a conference room. Where lighting controls are on override and you are not able to turn them off, talk to your building manager about changing the settings so you can use lighting as you need it.

11.5 Lighting controls

Motion sensors are great for storage areas, washrooms, and other areas that have periods of vacancy throughout the day. These sensors have shown to save 15 to 50 percent of lighting energy consumption. Installing motion sensors in parking garages can be excellent energy savers, as these areas are often lit 24/7.

Photocells are great for outdoor lighting systems. The photocell adjusts the lighting levels to meet light levels outside. They will automatically turn on at night and turn off when adequate sunlight is available. Some photocells have mechanisms to prevent temporary cloud cover from turning on the lights.

Dimmers allow for light level adjustments that make for a comfortable work space while reducing energy. Reducing light levels can also alleviate glare on computer screens. Some dimmers are not compatible with fluorescent and compact fluorescent bulbs — check the operating guidelines to be sure that a dimmer will work with your lighting system.

11.5a Types of lighting

There are a variety of choices when it comes to lighting. These options vary in the quality of light they generate, energy use, and life span. Lighting types with longer life spans reduce wasted energy and saves on maintenance costs. This can make more expensive lighting worth it in the long run. (See Table 7.)

11.5b Magnetic versus electronic ballasts

Light ballasts are very important to the function of fluorescent lamps. They are essentially small devices fit between the tube and the electrical current and function to control the amount of current through the tube.

If you have ever been annoyed by the flicker in your fluorescent lamps, or noticed an agonizing buzzing sound, you likely have old magnetic ballasts. Switching to electronic ballasts have many benefits and it is relatively cheap to do. Electronic ballasts are more sophisticated and eliminate the flicker and buzzing sound. These ballasts are also preferred because they cause less resistance to electricity flow and improve energy efficiency.

GREEN INNOVATION: The Next Big Thing in Lighting

Still in the early stages of development, OLEDs, or Organic Light Emitting Diodes, are made from organic materials and are ultra-durable. Not widely available on the market yet, OLEDs may be part of our future solutions to light technology.

11.6 LED exit signs

Exit signs typically have continual operating hours, making these big energy users. Often overlooked, conventional incandescent exit signs can be costly components of your energy bill. With notable energy savings and long life spans, LED exit signs are worth the upgrade. You may upgrade your current exit signs with a retrofit kit to reduce waste and cost. These typically pay back in less than six months.

11.7 Working with your landlord

If you lease your office space, electricity may be included in your monthly rental fees. Common in leased office space is a triple-net rental agreement that takes an average of the energy consumption for all office spaces and charges each tenant based on square footage. This can prevent tenants from tackling energy efficiency. In

Table 7
Lighting Types

Lighting Type	Description
Incandescent	Incandescent bulbs turn the majority of the energy they use into heat, with only a fraction being converted to light energy. This is what makes incandescent bulbs inefficient. These bulbs also have a relatively short life span of approximately 1,000 to 1,500 hours. In many countries, incandescent bulbs are being phased out and replaced with CFL or LED options.
Halogen/Zenon	Halogen or Zenon bulbs are incandescent with a tungsten filament and inert gas. They produce more light with less wattage when compared to regular incandescents but are still inefficient when compared to fluorescent or LED lighting.
LED (Light emitting diode)	LED bulbs are highly efficient and long-lasting. Compared to incandescent, LEDs can reduce energy consumption by 80 to 90 percent and last 50,000 to 100,000 hours. This can be 20 years of lighting! Although the price tag of $10 to $35 for a single bulb can be frightening, these bulbs are a smart investment. Cost has already come down significantly since they were first introduced to the market.
CFL (Compact Fluorescent)*	CFL bulbs (also known as pig's tail bulbs) are coiled fluorescent tubes in the shape of a bulb. They are an economical solution, as they use about a quarter of the energy compared to an incandescent and last many times longer — typically around 10,000 hours. These bulbs cost more than incandescents, but far less than LEDs. They result in cost savings after approximately 500 to 1,000 hours of use.
Fluorescent Tubes*	Common overhead lighting, fluorescent tubes come in a range of models that vary in efficiency. The T12 model is a wider tube and consumes a high volume of energy. T12s can be replaced with T8 or T5 models, which can reduce energy by up to 50 percent. The T8 and T5 models also improve light quality. Fluorescent tube lighting can also be replaced with LED track lighting or new tube-like technologies. **Note:** Switching from T12 to T5 bulbs or LED requires new fixtures.

* Fluorescent lighting contains small amounts of mercury and should be disposed of properly to avoid ecological contamination. Look into your local recycling services to find the best solution and make sure staff know the importance of proper disposal.

these cases it is the landlord — not the tenant — that benefits from the reduced utility costs.

You may have to work with your landlord to arrange these upgrades and agree on a way to share the cost savings or upgrade costs.

12. Windows

The building envelope of our physical buildings create a separation between the inside (conditioned) and outside (unconditioned) environment in which we live and work. We use our buildings to shelter us from changes in outdoor temperatures and climate, such as air, wind, water, and heat in a way that allows us to be comfortable in our surroundings.

One of the major considerations for this is the building structure and how well it is sealed and insulated from exposure to the outside environment. Although the walls, siding, and roofs are an important part of this, one common area that can increase our exposure to the outside environment is windows. Windows are great at allowing us to regulate heat in times when there may be an excess indoors and allow us access to fresh, cooler air from outside. Conversely, when we heat our spaces, air loss is most likely to occur in two ways: from air gaps around windows and through windows that have a high rate of heat transfer. This can result in substantial heat loss in colder seasons, or heat gain in times of excess outdoor heat.

12.1 Purchasing new windows

You may be thinking to yourself, how am I supposed to know what types of windows to buy? Fortunately, there are some new specifications on the market that provide standards for window performance such as ENERGY STAR, which makes it easier to see how new windows compare with one another. With the ENERGY STAR program in mind, you can shop for new windows and compare them based on their rated efficiency and guidelines.

To get you versed in the language of efficient windows you will want to consider what is known as the U-Factor, which is a rate of heat transfer. The U-Factor of windows means that the lower value you see noted on a window, the better the window is at keeping heat inside the building. If you find yourself in an area that has cold winters, consider upgrading your old windows to improve the energy performance and comfort level.

When purchasing new windows you will also want to consider what is called the solar-heat gain of the windows. This is a measure of how well a window surface will block heat from the sun. For offices in warmer climates, look for windows that have a lower solar-heat coefficient. This will help you keep out heat by reflecting incoming heat from the sun (solar radiation) and reducing the cost of cooling your office. Conversely, in cold climates you may want to take advantage of incoming solar radiation by purchasing windows with a higher solar-heat gain (or solar-heat coefficient) to take advantage of free heat from the sun. This is often referred to as passive heating.

12.2 Improving your existing windows

Another way to help reduce your exposure to the outside environment is by filling air gaps around your windows. Sealing your office windows with weather stripping is an easy way to save money on your heating bills while keeping you warm all winter long. Small gaps in windows may not seem like much but when you add them up throughout your entire office they can amount to a large hole roughly the size of a basketball. One way to check if you need to install weather stripping is to put your hand near the window on a windy day to see if you can feel air coming through. If so, it is time to go to the local hardware store and pick up some weather stripping. Applying weather stripping to your windows can be done quickly, easily, and affordably. The most common type of weather stripping is pressure-sensitive foam which has an adhesive back. These types of weather stripping are commonly installed on the top or bottom of a window. Follow these steps to help install the foam adhesive:

1. Clean the bottom of the window sill and window itself with warm water and dish detergent. This will ensure that when you go to attach the adhesive back it is secured properly.

2. Dry the cleaned windowsill and window where you will be applying the adhesive.

3. Measure the length of adhesive foam that you will need to apply and cut it to length. Scissors will work best.

4. Remove the thin layer of material that is attached to the adhesive back of the foam.

5. Apply the adhesive foam layer (the back) to the window and make sure that you press it firmly into place to secure it. **Note:** If there is any excess weather stripping sticking out, be sure to remove it so that you are not making the air gap worse off than when you found it!

6. Make sure that the window opens and closes properly and the next time it is windy, test if any air continues to get through.

Once you have completed this for one window you can repeat it with the rest of your office windows and doors to enhance your building envelope. If you are unable to get a good seal on your windows and doors, you may want to consider bringing in a professional to help you draft-proof.

13. Heating and Cooling

Although we have been through many of ways in which we can improve the environmental performance of your office building we have yet to touch on the single largest user of energy in the office and that is the heating and cooling. According to Natural Resources, Canada's Office of Energy Efficiency, commercial, industrial, and institutional buildings allocate 53 percent of their energy use for space heating and cooling. This is responsible for 7 percent of the total annual GHG emissions in Canada.

There are a few easy steps that you can take to start to manage your office heating and cooling. One of the first measures, mentioned in section **12.**, is to properly seal windows and doors in your office and ensure your space is properly insulated. It is recommended that you bring an insulation professional to your workspace to determine the current level of insulation and provide a set of recommendations for cost-effective ways in which you can improve the R-value of your office. This is a good starting place for reducing your energy use but it is not the only approach that you should consider. The rest of this section is dedicated to providing you with an understanding of how you can manage your office heating and cooling better, identify the ways in which you are currently heating your space, and improve the environmental performance of the heating options that you use.

13.1 Common office heating systems

Heating systems vary greatly in both heat source and how heat is distributed. Smaller offices may have baseboard heating that use electricity as the heating source. Although these are relatively efficient, how your electricity is being generated may not be. Your city may use coal, nuclear, hydro, or other electricity scources. One way to offset this is through the purchase of clean energy or green energy sources such as wind, biomass, or solar.

Larger offices or those in leased spaces within larger buildings may have centralized heating systems that use boilers and furnaces to heat air which is distributed throughout your office. These systems may be relatively efficient at heating space when compared to conventional baseboard systems; however, many use fuels that have high GHG emissions factors such as oil, diesel, natural gas, or propane. Cooling your office space is typically provided through the use of centralized air conditioning units that run on electricity. There is a wide array of air conditioning unit types, but their role is to lower the air temperature through a refrigeration cycle or evaporation which cools air that is then distributed to your office space. The common name for a completed system of heating, ventilation, and air conditioning is known as an HVAC system. These systems are typically centralized throughout a facility.

13.2 Managing your office's heating and cooling system

Now that you have looked further into how your office space is heated and cooled it is important to look at how you can prevent energy waste by improving the way you manage your offices HVAC system. In some cases it is difficult for organizations that lease space to get access to appropriate heating controls. In these cases, the property managers or landlords are responsible for ensuring that the building HVAC system is maintained. As noted in several other sections, it is very important to work with your landlords or property managers to ensure that you are able to run an efficient business operation that benefits your staff and clients while protecting the environment and reducing costs.

In many offices, HVAC is controlled through manual thermostats. Although these are great because you can easily access them to make heating and cooling changes, it is also easy for others in your office to turn up the dial if they feel cold or down if they are feeling too hot. Chances are you are not going to be able to make everyone happy but the best approach is to install a programmable thermostat. This will allow you to set time and temperature settings for your baseboard and/or centralized HVAC unit. This is especially important for conserving energy outside regular office hours when no one is in the office space.

The following are key things to consider when purchasing a programmable thermostat:

1. How many temperature settings will it allow you to set in a day? You will want to be sure that you can change the temperature settings at least twice a day to coincide with the start and end of your office work days.

2. Make sure that it allows you to adjust the heating or air conditioning on and off times as the outside temperature changes.

3. Purchase a model that will let you save daily settings and repeat them as needed.

4. Finally, set the system to start an hour before you open the office to make sure that it is comfortable for staff on their arrival. Remember, the ideal temperatures for an occupied space are 21 degrees Celsius or 71 degrees Fahrenheit. When getting the system ready to be shut down for the night you can set the temperature to turn down a half hour before the office is closed as it will take some time to warm up or to cool down. The ideal temperature to set it to when unoccupied is 15 degrees Celsius or 61 degrees Fahrenheit.

Note: These temperature ranges may vary depending on the heating system type, efficiency levels, and outside temperatures. Be sure to consult with your HVAC professional on the desired temperature range when occupied and unoccupied in order to make sure that you are maximizing the efficiency of your HVAC system. In colder climates, be sure to maintain temperatures to avoid burst pipes in the winter.

When considering the way that you cool your office space, it is important to know that older systems, those ten years old or older should be considered ready for an upgrade. Air conditioning units have greatly improved in energy-efficiency ratings and with the amount that you can save on your energy bills annually they will likely have a quick payback. Look for the ENERGY STAR label to help you purchase an energy-efficient unit that will save money and reduce air pollution.

When in doubt, hire an HVAC professional for technical advice. There are many system configurations that can help improve the performance of your HVAC system but individuals with professional training and experience will ensure that your system is running and maintained in a way that helps you save money while helping to protect the environment.

13.3 Staff education

Staff behavior can dramatically impact the performance of your building and the amount of energy it consumes. If your office is often too hot, then it may be a good idea to relax the dress code in times of extreme heat or during the summer months. Although this may seem like a no-brainer, it is often not considered. This simple change can help lower the cost of cooling the space in the hottest months of the year, and make your staff more comfortable.

Conversely, if you are finding that your office heating bills are skyrocketing in the winter, it may be a good idea to promote sweater wearing and drop the thermostat setting a few degrees to save energy. Get your office green team involved and come up with some fun and creative ways to do this during the holiday season (e.g., ugly sweater contest) and give out some prizes. It might be a $10 gift certificate for your local coffee shop or sandwich joint; little incentives can go a long way in encouraging people to participate. Once again, support from the top is key for these fun and engaging initiatives. Many people may not take it seriously until upper management sends a memo with a picture of the ugly Christmas sweater he or she will be wearing and names the prize for the winner (as decided on by staff). Do it once and people around the office may make it an annual tradition.

If you have multiple offices, you could hold an energy-savings contest where you track your energy from the previous year and compete against each office to see which one can save the most energy. Provide staggered incentive rates or prizes to encourage greater savings. The key is to make it fun and engaging and celebrate staff successes.

14. Furniture

Furniture options are about as diverse as it comes, but there is an evident spectrum of green to not-so-green types of furniture available. To make environmentally friendly choices, you will need to understand how different products are made and what components have a high environmental impact.

Here are a few ideas to consider for your green furniture choices:

1. Give old pieces a new life. The greenest piece of furniture is an existing one. There are many great, high-quality pieces that need freshening up to give them a second life. You can reupholster, refinish, or rebuild furniture to keep your environmental impact and costs low.

   Example: A Victoria-based accounting firm had some old oak desks and had the tops remade and the frames painted white to give them a new look and a new life.

2. Wood and alternatives: Wood is a natural and renewable furniture option, but deforestation is happening at a rapid pace, causing further global warming, and loss of habitat and soil erosion. Globally, 13 million hectares are deforested each year. When buying new furniture, look for the Forest Stewardship Council (FSC) stamp to assure the new piece you are buying is made from sustainably harvested wood.

   Bamboo and cork are both renewable options for furniture components. Bamboo is fast growing and cork can be harvested annually from the bark of the cork tree, without killing the tree.

3. Steer clear of VOCs: Avoid furniture made from pressed sawdust and glue to avoid the toxic emissions they release. Often cheap products like this have high VOC content with chemicals such as formaldehyde that become airborne, reducing air quality. Greenguard is a certification that assures the furniture has low toxicity.

4. Recycled components: Mining raw earth and oil to make furniture components puts great pressures on finite resources. Furniture made of recycled content, such as plastic and metal, will have a reduced environmental impact. Look for information on the product specs that state how much of the product is made from recycled materials.

5. Buy furniture that is built to last: When a chair is built with flimsy plastic, low-quality metal screws, and fabric that wears thin, it is not going to last long. Higher quality components usually mean a higher price tag, but think of them as investments. It can be worth it to buy great, long-lasting pieces that can endure years and years of use. Go for durable. Furniture that is built to last is designed to be disassembled for repair when needed. Items that are an inseparable mash of wood, plastic, metal, and glue are often destined for the landfill. Look for the Cradle2Cradle logo, which verifies the product was designed with its entire life cycle in mind.

6. Keep it modular: Modular systems offer flexibility for new office arrangements. Your business may expand or contract and need to make changes to how your space is oriented. Modular systems include workstations that can have sections added or removed and even walls that can be moved to shift divided areas. These systems can last longer because they can change as your business does, rather than needing to replace old furniture with new pieces.

7. Make furniture of reclaimed materials: Furniture that was made from reclaimed wood is a green choice. You may be able to find local woodworkers who will use these materials to custom build your environmentally friendly furniture. While this may not be practical for all of your furniture, a few feature pieces will add style and uniqueness to your office.

Case Study: At our office, Synergy Enterprises, we help companies measure their carbon footprint and green their operations. Naturally, we wanted to build a super-green office to be a case study for our clients. We found a woodworker who founded a company called WoodCoast, which specializes in using reclaimed wood from demolition houses for custom furniture and construction. Though we did not have endless cash to spend on furniture, we were able to get three desks made out of solid, recycled wood for a price comparable to a new, mid-range desk from a distributor. We place a higher value on these desks because they are solid and could last for generations. You can literally jump on them and they don't move. (Doesn't everyone test their furniture that way?) Furthermore, the desks have a story. The wood for one desk came from an old home in town, another from a demolished air hanger. It felt good to be supporting a local company that is working to make a difference.

15. Renovations

The best time to start to make green changes is during renovations. The decisions you make during the design phase can be more cost effective than making changes while your office is in full-operating mode.

Take Farley Martin Notary Public for example; this small office of five staff decided to go green when they were moving to a new office space. They needed to complete the space with drywall, flooring, furniture, plumbing fixtures, and more. The owners hired JC Scott Ecodesign and chose construction materials, fixtures, and furniture that fit their vision of a green office. Every toilet and faucet is a low-flow model, the lighting is LED or high-efficiency fluorescent, the flooring includes eco-friendly carpets that can be recycled and natural linoleum, the desks were purchased used or reused from their previous office space. When you enter the office, the first thing you see is a living green wall, giving the office a fresh, modern, and eco-friendly first impression. Signage around the space describes the various green aspects of their office: "This copy machine is set to double-sided printing, which will save over 80 trees every year." The business has been featured in local magazines and newspapers for their office renovation and commitment to the environment.

Depending on the depth of your office renovation, you can design your space to maximize natural light, improve energy efficiency, reduce water consumption, improve air quality, and reduce your impact on the planet by making green furniture and finishing choices. Whether your renovation is large or small, use this window of opportunity to make a positive impact on employee health while reducing your environmental impact.

15.1 Framing

On the design side, employ framing methods such as Advanced Wall Framing, which uses less wood and makes room for more insulation to improve your building energy efficiency. These building approaches can help you meet building code and structural requirements without wasting materials.

Whether you are using wood, steel, or another option for framing your walls, there are green options. For wood framing, choosing products certified by the Forest Stewardship Council (FSC) will ensure that the wood was sustainably harvested. You can also look at using some recycled or reclaimed wood, which would offset your need for new products, but make sure your local building code will allow this.

15.2 Drywall

Typical drywall consists of gypsum, a product that is mined and calcified using heat. This cooking process commonly uses natural gas, which has a carbon footprint associated with it, so it is important to use drywall with recycled content and waste as little as possible during your installation. A study in Wisconsin found that 17 percent of drywall is wasted during the manufacturing and installation process. An eco-friendly option is to buy drywall with recycled content. New brands of green drywall options are emerging with options for 100 percent recycled face and back paper and recycled gypsum or synthetic gypsum made from a byproduct of another industrial process.

15.3 Insulation

Insulation is important for creating thermal and sound barriers where they are needed. As energy costs have risen, so has the need to properly insulate homes and buildings. The R-value, ranging from R1 to R60 or so, will tell you how well it can resist heat. Insulation is typically made from fiberglass, which is made by using a multi-stage, high-heat manufacturing process that has a high carbon footprint, compared to greener alternatives. Alternative insulation products such as cellulose fibre, sheep wool, cotton, and shredded blue jean fabric are renewable, naturally derived, and biodegradable and can have a far lower carbon footprint than fiberglass insulation.

15.4 Modular systems

Investing in modular-wall systems to create dividers within your office space can help you avoid demolitions later. Modular systems can change configurations as needed and provide similar aspects of thermal and sound insulation. While modular systems can be more expensive, they become an asset rather than a leasehold improvement and can be resold or moved to a new space if needed.

15.5 Flooring

There was a myth going around that cork was endangered. We learned recently that this is not the case. Cork forests could actually become at risk if we do not continue the cork market, because other farming practices will come in and tear down the trees. What makes cork forests so remarkable, and sustainable, is they can be harvested while still supporting a thriving ecology of birds, insects, and other animals. Cork flooring also offers added comfort and thermal insulation.

Traditional linoleum, still made today, consists of organic materials such as pine resin, flour, linseed oil, and pigment. However, similar products are made with non-organic vinyl material. Polyvinyl chloride (PVC) offers brighter colors, but is made from non-renewable resources and can contain substances such as phthalate plasticizers, which are a major health concern. You may see the name "marmoleum" as well. This is the name of a product from Forbo Flooring, one of the largest linoleum manufacturers, which is based in Europe and makes true linoleum products.

One clothing company, Hemp & Company, located in downtown Victoria, recently renovated their new space. Wanting it to be as green as possible, they discovered fir beams in an old building and had them milled into floor boards. They finished the floors with a natural stain that will not emit high levels of air pollutants.

Polished concrete is becoming more popular in retail spaces, restaurants, and even offices. Worldwide, our consumption of concrete is a major contributor to CO_2 emissions. A key component of concrete is cement. The cement-manufacturing process alone contributes to more than 5 percent of global greenhouse gas emissions, and this is due to its mass production. However, concrete can be made locally, which results in fewer transportation emissions than, say, bamboo flooring from another continent. In addition, concrete offers valuable thermal properties as it can absorb and store heat, reducing the need for insulation.

Natural carpet options have fibres from jute, wool, cotton, and coconut husk. Carpet tiles have become popular solutions because the tiles can be replaced in areas of heavy wear, rather than replacing entire large sections. One company, Interface Flooring, has made strides towards revolutionizing the carpet manufacturing process to make its carpet recyclable into new carpet.

15.6 Painting

Water-based paints have become popular over the past few decades, phasing out the use of oil-based paint, which typically has higher levels of Volatile Organic Compounds (VOCs).

Choosing green paint options can significantly improve your office air quality and reduce your environmental impact. There is a growing awareness that VOCs are released from new paint, adding harmful substances to the air you breathe. New options of paint are available at most conventional home renovation or paint stores with low or zero VOCs.

There are also options that use naturally derived, biodegradable pigments, such as Milk Paint which is made from milk protein, lime, clay, and natural pigments.

15.7 Construction waste

The amount of wood, concrete, metal, drywall, and plastic that enters construction waste bins is incredible. Many of these materials will be recyclable at one of your local facilities. The key is sorting it. Communicate with your contractor or construction crew that you want all the waste to be recycled properly, rather than having a catch-all bin that goes straight to the dump, full of reusable and compostable materials.

9
Making Your Office Carbon Neutral

1. *Measuring Your Carbon Footprint*

One way to gain an understanding of how your business is impacting the environment is to measure the total annual carbon footprint of your operations. The greenhouse gas protocol is the recognized international standard for measuring carbon footprints.

For any type of business, the carbon footprint is divided into three scopes. Scope 1 is direct emissions, resulting from combustion of fossil fuels in property and vehicles the company owns or leases. Scope 2 is indirect emissions from electricity consumption and Scope 3 is indirect emission sources that occur at other companies or locations, but are influenced by your business. Here is a list of emission sources common to most office-type businesses:

Scope 1: Direct emissions

    Fuel used in company-owned or leased vehicles.

    Oil or natural gas (commonly used for heating).

    Propane or other fuel purchased.

Scope 2: Indirect emissions from energy

Electricity consumed by space you own or lease.

Scope 3: Other indirect emissions

Water used (e.g., washrooms, kitchens).

Waste produced.

Paper purchased.

Fuel from deliveries or service calls.

Flights, hotels, and taxis paid for by the company.

Employee commuting (fuel).

The carbon footprints of companies in manufacturing, transportation, and construction sectors dwarf those that occur in office-based businesses; however, the quantity of office-based businesses adds up to a significant impact on the planet and global warming. The built environment is a huge part of North America's total carbon footprint, as is transportation.

One of the first organizations to help companies measure their greenhouse-gas emissions was Climate Smart™. This social enterprise is now able to benchmark individual businesses against their growing set of data on office-based operations.

In a study of 236 office-based businesses, Climate Smart determined an average carbon emissions profile. Most of these businesses were located in Western Canada, which explains the low-emissions profile for electricity. Most of British Columbia is powered by hydroelectricity, which has a low carbon footprint when compared to coal-fired energy.

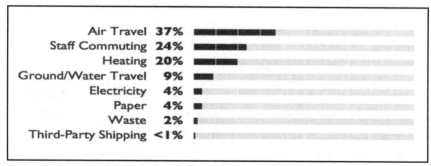

Figure 5: Average carbon footprint of an office-based company.
Source: Climate Smart Business Inc., 2013. "Offices and Carbon Emissions: An Industry Brief."

Each source of emissions has a conversion factor to determine its carbon footprint. You will need to gather the raw data for the emission sources you decide to report on, such as liters of fuel, miles or kilometers of air travel, and reams of paper. You can then use a carbon calculator, such as the EPA Greenhouse Gas Equivalency Calculator (USA) or the CarbonZero Carbon Emissions Calculator (USA or Canada) to determine your total carbon footprint.

If you would like support to complete your carbon footprint report, you can use online software programs such as GobiSOFT or Climate Smart, or hire an environmental consulting firm such as Synergy Enterprises (yes, that was a plug, but it's the only one, we promise) to gather the data and produce a report.

Case Study: Monk Office

Monk Office is a company that services businesses on Vancouver Island with office products and technology. They have been measuring the carbon footprint of its head office and distribution center since 2010. With an effort to green its operations, it has reduced its carbon footprint from 218 tonnes of CO_2 in 2007 to 47 tonnes of CO_2 in 2012, a 78.5 percent reduction over the course of six years. It achieved this by focusing on areas that had the largest carbon footprint: natural gas, waste generation, electricity, and paper. This company is a fantastic example of how incremental, consistent changes can add up to a big win for the environment. The company now carr\ies environmentally friendly products, has won several environmental awards, and has been featured in textbooks, conferences, and classrooms as a case study for how to go green.

"It all started with the recycling. We wanted to reduce our waste and were trying to find better recycling solutions," said Debbie Schultz, Executive Assistant to the CEO of Monk Office and member of the Monk Office Eco Team. "We started with the simple things, but it led to changing how we do business entirely. We now recycle everything — even organics, soft plastics, batteries, Styrofoam, and pallets."

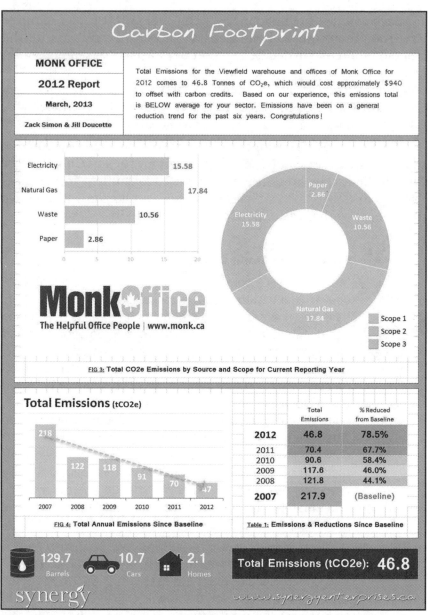

Figure 6: Summary of Carbon Footprint Report for Monk Office Head Office and Distribution Center.
(Source: EPA Clean Energy, Greenhouse Gas Equivalencies Calculator, 2014)

How do you visualize what a tonne of carbon dioxide equivalent (CO_2) looks like? A single tonne of CO_2 is equivalent to the following:

- Driving an average passenger vehicle 2,381 miles.
- 113 gallons of gasoline combusted.
- 1,074 pounds of coal combusted.
- 42 household BBQ propane cylinders combusted.

Measuring your footprint can give you a baseline from which to measure future performance metrics. While it takes effort, you will gain valuable insight into how your office is operating and where your greatest opportunities are to reduce impact on climate change and global warming.

For more on measuring your carbon footprint check out a publication by the World Resource Institute called "Working 9-5 on Climate Change: An Office Guide."

2. Carbon Credits

After you have reduced your office's emissions as much as possible, you may choose to purchase carbon credits to become carbon neutral. A carbon credit is created when money is invested in a project that physically eliminates the output of carbon into the atmosphere. There is often a great deal of confusion around what a carbon credit is, because carbon credits exist in a spectrum of quality. It is important that the credits you purchase be third-party verified to a reputable standard such as Verified Carbon Standard (VCS) or Gold Standard (GS).

To be a verified carbon credit, the project must go through a rigorous review which ensures the project a) would not have otherwise occurred without the investment; b) will have a lasting, permanent effect; c) is measurably reducing carbon emissions; and d) is never double-counted. This and other criteria allow the project to become a carbon credit, adding it to a pot from which companies can purchase to offset their emissions and become certified carbon neutral.

In essence, buying carbon credits supports new, emerging green technologies that reduce carbon emissions. It may not be possible for your company to reach zero emissions. You may need to drive, or have an office space that uses computers. By purchasing carbon credits, you are taking full responsibility for the emissions you create as a company and are investing into projects that will reduce the same quantity of emissions you create. Carbon credits are an important component of a green economy because it allows for projects that may not make a great immediate financial payback to take place in the market. For example, a school may not have the capital to invest in a heat pump that will reduce emissions from its heating system but if it is provided with carbon credits for the amount of carbon that will be reduced as a result of purchasing the heat pump, it may become affordable.

10
Marketing

When you start to see your garbage dwindle, your energy bills plummet, and new green products in your office, you may think, "Gee, we should start telling people what we are doing here!" You may also be wondering, "How should we go about telling people we are green without being pompous?" or "When will we have accomplished enough to start talking about being green?" The ideal time to promote your achievements is when you have results in the form of metrics or visual environmental changes to share. It is also valuable to share stories of the challenges your business overcame to go green.

Marketing your business as a green company can have many benefits. First and foremost, you will attract the conscious consumer base that is driven to select products and services according to their environmental values. As people become more educated and aware of environmental issues, consumer patterns change accordingly. When I was in my third year of university, I enrolled in Environmental Studies 100, a class that presented an overview of environmental issues. The class had room for 60 students and was offered once per year. It barely met the minimum registration numbers required to continue. In 2014, that same class has room for

250 students and is offered six times per year. I returned ten years after I had taken the class to give a guest lecture. Remembering my past experience in the class, I thought there would be a few dozen of us sitting on the grass somewhere. I sure wasn't expecting a couple hundred environmental keeners. We have seen tremendous growth in the interest of this topic, not just in the classroom, but in consumer patterns as well. A study by Carolyn Strong has found a similar trend:

"The increasingly well-informed consumer is not only demanding fairly traded products, but is challenging manufacturers and retailers to guarantee the ethical claims they are making about their products." (*Saving Water in Office Buildings*, US EPA, 2010.)

Making information about your environmental values and actions available to the public can also strengthen your relationships with existing customers. They may already use your company's service, or buy your product, but there is value in enhancing their experience and giving them a reason to feel good about choosing your company over your competitors. It may be the reason they stick with you, instead of switching. The feel-good effect you get when you buy from a company that shares your values is difficult to measure, but we know it is a powerful motivator for customer loyalty and that is worth a lot more than most advertising campaigns.

1. *Ways to Promote Your Achievements*

Here is a list of ways you could promote your office achievements:

1. Use social media to communicate changes in your workplace and results.

2. Add a page to your website that discussess your environmental values and practices.

3. Create posters with information to post in your lobby and washrooms.

4. Apply for environmental business and/or innovation awards.

5. Go for a green business certification.

6. Engage the media — send press releases and write letters to the editor

7. Write blog posts on how you overcame challenges to go green.

8. Include sustainability information in your flyers, pamphlets, and other materials.

9. Publish a Corporate Social Responsibility Report.

10. Do speaking engagements to classrooms, peer businesses, and associations on the topic of green busines practices.

2. Greenwashing

If you are someone who tries to shop green, you have probably been duped by some "green product" that wasn't all that environmentally friendly. Maybe it was a cleaning product that had a label depicting foliage and images of nature, or a toxic product with slightly less packaging. This marketing maneuver is called greenwashing. Companies do this because they know more consumers care about the environment, and they want their product to meet their customers' values, without having to go through major changes. Words like "natural," "eco," and "green" are used quite freely in marketing, so it is best to educate yourself on how to read labels and know what is behind a green certification.

For many businesses we have worked with, their greatest fear is that they will be seen as greenwashers for marketing their efforts. They, too, have been annoyed with greenwashed products and services and have felt a sense of betrayal towards a company or brand for its lack of honesty. The last thing they want is for their customers to feel that way towards them. For this reason, many companies engage in the opposite sin, termed greenhushing. In this case, companies completely close up and don't discuss environmental performance whatsoever. If you have this same concern, we encourage you, as we have with other companies, to tell the public what your business is doing to be more environmentally friendly. First and foremost, it will have a positive impact on your brand and customer loyalty. This can be the greatest benefit to greening your business. There is another reason to market your green efforts: You will be raising the bar for your industry and setting an example of responsible business practices. You can start to change business-as-usual in your sector and lead the way towards a more sustainable future.

Greenwashing has indeed increased consumer skepticism, but you can gain and maintain consumer confidence by communicating your environmental performance with transparency and clarity. The following principals will keep your business accountable and allow you to market your products or practices without greenwashing:

1. **Be transparent:** Talk about the wins and the losses, your strengths and your weaknesses.

2. **Be specific:** Speak to what your business actually achieved. Avoid general terms such as "we are a green business." What made you green? What actions are backing this self-proclamation? What were the results? Do you have any numbers or metrics to show?

3. **Be real:** Use the human element. Draw on the values of your company. Why did you decide to go green? What was your inspiration? What were the challenges?

4. **Make it visual:** Paint a picture of what you are doing, use graphs and charts (but keep them simple), use infographics. Post the results where people can see and make it visually engaging.

See Figure 7 for an example of how to display your initiatives. This Corporate Social Responsibility infographic is used at Inn at Laurel Point to communicate to guests, employees, and partner organizations. The graphic is used in print format and on its website.

3. Greenhushing

The opposite of greenwashing is termed "greenhushing." This occurs when a business has great values, practices, and policies, but does not communicate this to its customers and in many cases, not even to its staff.

Without transparency and active communication a company could be greenhushing and missing out on the opportunity to enhance its brand. In addition, companies who do talk about their environmental and social performance start ripple effects that impact their employees, peer businesses, suppliers, and customers. A good example of this is Habit Coffee, an independently owned coffee shop in Victoria, BC. When this small coffee shop decided to go green, it was based on the values of the owner, Shane Devereaux, who said, "I just want to do it because it's the right thing to do, I don't want to use it in marketing." A year later, I convinced him to put up a poster in his business. This was a simple poster that outlined what actions the business had taken to reduce environmental impact and give back to the community. Habit Coffee put these posters at the exits, in the washrooms, and at the till (see Figure 8, Habit Coffee Go Green Poster, Version 1, 2011).

Figure 7: Inn at Laurel Point Corporate Social Responsibility infographic; an example of how to visually display your initiatives.

The simple act of letting your customers and staff know what is happening behind the scenes creates trust and company loyalty.

A number of other business owners frequent this coffee shop and saw the GO GREEN poster. Inspired, they started their own sustainability programs. These businesses included a brew pub, an accounting firm, and a construction company.

The ripple effects from your marketing and education may be unknown, but you can be sure that your business will be setting an example for how to create positive change in the world, from within your office.

Figure 8: Habit Coffee Go Green Poster, Version 1, 2011.

Conclusion

If you can green your business, improve your working environment for your staff, save costs, and gain exposure, you have truly developed a strong, triple-bottom-line business.

Synergy's green business model with the four key phases to assess, engage, implement, and market has proven successful for dozens of businesses and it can work for your office too.

We hope you have gained valuable insight and tips through the chapters of this book.

We truly believe that businesses will change the world and help us reach a more sustainable future. Your efforts may seem small and inconsequential in the vast sphere of environmental turmoil, but we assure you, every action creates a ripple effect and your small actions can amount to tidal waves of change.

We encourage you to share what you have learned in this book and work with your team to ingrain environmental values into the way you do business. Think critically, look for better solutions, and continually innovate.

To a healthier planet and your fantastic business.

Jill Doucette and Lee Johnson

Download Kit

Please enter the URL you see in the box below into your computer web browser to access and download the kit.

www.self-counsel.com/updates/greenoffice/14kit.htm

The kit includes References and Resources for Further Reading as well as the following checklists:

- Green Office Assessment
- Assess Your Cleaning Products
- Eight Questions to Ask Your Catering Company
- Waste Audit
- Questions to Ask Your Recycling Provider
- Energy Audit